SURVIVING THE FALLOUT: A COMPLETE FAMILY GUIDE TO NUCLEAR CRISIS PREPAREDNESS

MASTERING ESSENTIAL STRATEGIES FOR PROTECTION, PSYCHOLOGICAL RESILIENCE, AND SUSTAINED SURVIVAL IN NUCLEAR EMERGENCIES

TED RILEY

Copyright © 2025 Ted Riley. - All rights reserved.

The content contained within this book may not be reproduced, duplicated, or transmitted without direct written permission from the author or the publisher.

Under no circumstances will any blame or legal responsibility be held against the publisher, or author, for any damages, reparation, or monetary loss due to the information contained within this book, either directly or indirectly.

Legal Notice:

This book is copyright protected. It is only for personal use. You cannot amend, distribute, sell, use, quote, or paraphrase any part, or the content within this book, without the consent of the author or publisher.

Disclaimer Notice:

Please note the information contained within this document is for educational and entertainment purposes only. All effort has been executed to present accurate, up to date, reliable, complete information. No warranties of any kind are declared or implied. Readers acknowledge that the author is not engaged in the rendering of legal, financial, medical, or professional advice. The content within this book has been derived from various sources. Please consult a licensed professional before attempting any techniques outlined in this book.

By reading this document, the reader agrees that under no circumstances is the author responsible for any losses, direct or indirect, that are incurred as a result of the use of the information contained within this document, including, but not limited to, errors, omissions, or inaccuracies.

ISBN Paperback: 978-0-6486411-9-3

ISBN Hardback: 978-1-923521-00-1

CONTENTS

Introduction	7
1. WHAT ARE WE WORRYING ABOUT? THE POTENTIAL DANGERS AHEAD	11
Nuclear Weapons	12
Nuclear Power	15
Take Action!	18
2. AND THEN WHAT? THE EFFECTS OF NUCLEAR FALLOUT AND RADIATION	19
The Truth About Nuclear Waste	20
The Impact of a Nuclear Attack	26
The Impact of a Nuclear War	28
Physical Health Isn't Our Only Concern	33
Take Action!	34
3. STAYING SAFE … AS FAR INSIDE AS YOU CAN GET	37
Shelter or Evacuate?	37
Finding Suitable Shelter	39
Fallout Shelters	40
Where to Go After the Fallout	46
Take Action!	47
4. BE PREPARED! WHAT YOU CAN DO TO GET READY NOW	49
What Should Be Inside Your Shelter	50
Training Yourself for Survival	60
Take Action!	87
5. THE CONVERSATIONS NO ONE WANTS TO HAVE—HOW TO PREPARE YOUR FAMILY	91
Talking About Survival	92
Training Your Family	96
What To Do When They Don't Take It Seriously	99
Talking About Nuclear Disasters	100

Dealing With Anxiety	102
Take Action!	102

6. MAYDAY! WHAT TO DO AS SOON AS YOU LEARN OF A NUCLEAR DISASTER — 105

Hearing About the Disaster	105
What to Do Immediately	107
Navigating the Immediate Issues	109
Take Action!	115

7. STAY ALERT—SURVIVAL FOR THE FIRST FEW MONTHS — 117

Sheltering in Place	117
Evacuation	121
Managing the Psychological Impact	123
Take Action!	126

8. THE NEW NORMAL—STRATEGIES FOR LONG-TERM SURVIVAL — 129

Could You Go Home?	130
Food Production	133
Water	136
Social Aspects	137
Psychological Health	141
Take Action!	144

9. PRIORITY #1—PROTECTING YOUR HEALTH IN A POST-NUCLEAR WORLD — 147

Radiation Sickness	147
Short Term Safety	150
Nutrition	151
Physical Fitness	154
Mental Resilience	156
Protecting Mental Health	159
Hygiene	160
The Reality of a Nuclear Winter	161
Take Action!	162

10. THE WORST-CASE SCENARIO—POST-
    INCIDENT RECOVERY   165
    Rebuilding   165
    Surviving Amid the Chaos   167
    Take Action!   170

    Conclusion   173
    Answers for Chapter 2 Quiz   175
    References   185

A Special Gift to My Readers

Included with your purchase of this book is your free copy of the *Emergency Information Planner*

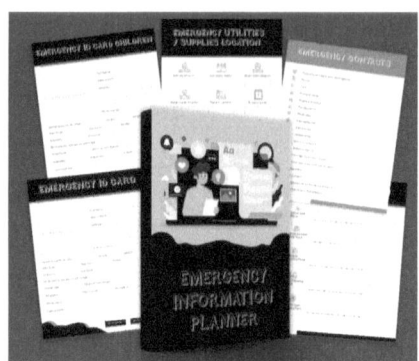

Follow the link below to receive your copy:
www.tedrileyauthor.com
Or by accessing the QR code:

You can also join our Facebook community **Suburban Prepping with Ted**, or contact me directly via ted@tedrileyauthor.com.

INTRODUCTION

"It wasn't raining when Noah built the ark."

— RICHARD CUSHING

In April 2024, there was a series of attacks focused on the Zaporizhzhia Power Plant in Ukraine. Perhaps you were reading the news at that time, and if you were, you probably found this as alarming as I did. In the wake of those attacks, the UN warned the Security Council that if there were to be a war anywhere near a major nuclear power program like this, there would be a very high chance of a nuclear accident (United Nations 2024). That's frightening enough, but it all levels up a notch once we start to bring nuclear weapons into the equation. Just one of these weapons has the power to completely destroy a city and kill most of its inhabitants. If there were to be a series of nuclear explosions affecting multiple cities, this could end the lives of tens of millions of people. For those who survived, the health consequences would be very serious, and we'd be facing severe climate change with devastating consequences of its own (The International Campaign to Abolish Nuclear Weapons (ICAN) n.d.). Sadly, even if none of this ever happens, the chances of us seeing another incident like Chornobyl before 2050 are, according to safety specialists, about 50:50 (Emerging Technology from the ArXiv 2015).

It brings me no joy to open a book with such sobering information, but given that you're reading it, I'd assume that you, like me, are already concerned about this. The political landscape is worrying, to say the least, and we've never been more at risk of a nuclear war. Plus, although nuclear power production is much safer nowadays, it's still incredibly dangerous, and no one can rule out another disaster. I've been preparing for emergencies of all kinds for years, but if I'm being honest, nuclear risks had never really crossed my mind. As soon as they did, I realized I needed to do more to protect my family, and I'm sure this is what you're concerned about, too. You're worried about how you'll look after your mental and physical health if we find ourselves faced with a nuclear crisis, and you want to know what the dangers are so you can guard against them.

This is where I was, too, and I have good news and bad news for you. The good news is first because I always like to focus on hope: There are definitely things you can do to prepare for a nuclear emergency. The bad news is that there are some things that are very difficult to prepare for completely, and a full-blown nuclear war is one of them. We can be as prepared as we like, but we're still human, and, much to my son's irritation, we're not invincible. I tell you this because I want you to go into preparation realistically, and I want you to focus where it's most needed: on what you *can* do to protect your family. This is what I've been working on myself, and I intend to guide you through all the essential strategies you'll need to stay safe, keep up your mental resilience, and survive in the aftermath of a nuclear emergency.

I'm lucky enough to live on a homestead with a fair bit of space around it, but I know that your situation may be very different. My goal is for all the advice that you read here to be accessible no matter where you live or what your background is. My goal is for you to feel confident that you know what to do in a nuclear emergency. I can certainly tell you that I'm now more prepared for a nuclear crisis than I've ever been in the past, and much as watching the news alarms me, I'm confident that I can do everything in my power to protect my family. I know that's your priority, too, so let's not delay any further. Let's get started by considering the potential dangers that face us.

1

WHAT ARE WE WORRYING ABOUT? THE POTENTIAL DANGERS AHEAD

My own worries about nuclear disaster began in 2022 when Russia threatened to use nuclear weapons against Ukraine. Right from the start of Russia's invasion of Ukraine that year, Vladimir Putin was using this threat in an attempt to get Ukraine to give in to his country's demands (Dreuzy and Gilli 2022). I found my head flooded with "What if?" scenarios, and it got me thinking about nuclear dangers in general. I realized that even though some dangers are less pronounced than they used to be, there will always be risks in a world in which nuclear energy is produced. We could well see another nuclear accident from a power plant within our lifetime. We'll look at all of these dangers in this chapter because the first part of being prepared is knowing exactly what it is you're preparing for.

NUCLEAR WEAPONS

I think nuclear weapons are the most frightening part of what we're looking at here. They're the most dangerous weapons on the planet, and a single one has the power to wipe out a whole city, not only killing many of the people who live there but also leaving devastating effects that will last for a very long time afterward. Nuclear weapons have, so far, only ever been used twice in war. Both of these instances happened in 1945, during World War II, and you'll know of them as the bombings of Hiroshima and Nagasaki (U.N. n.d.). Although this has only happened twice, these weapons still exist, and as you'll see shortly, the risk of them being used again is higher than it's been in a long time.

Before we get to that, though, let's clarify exactly what a nuclear weapon is. There's obviously a lot of detail we could go into here, but for the purposes of being prepared, you need only a basic understanding. A nuclear weapon is any device that releases nuclear energy at a rapid rate. They're made when chemical explosives are combined with nuclear fission (which is caused by the explosives compressing nuclear material), which then releases a vast quantity of energy as X-rays. This, in turn, raises the pressure and temperature to heights great enough to ignite nuclear fusion. Modern nuclear weapons, therefore, involve both fission and fusion, which means that a single one of them is capable of releasing a huge amount of explosive energy in a split second—more than the two atom bombs used in World War II combined, which used only fission (Union of Concerned Scientists 2016).

Modern nuclear weapons also have a range of different delivery systems. They can be deployed by missiles, bombers, or submarines (known together as a nuclear triad), all three of which are included in the US's nuclear arsenal. It's also possible for a nuclear weapon to be delivered in another way, such as in a bag—a tactic more likely to be favored by a terrorist (DeNardi 2012). However, we're probably less at risk of this than we are of them being used by a government. Although extremist groups have threatened possible nuclear attacks, they haven't proved that they have these weapons, and if they have, they certainly haven't used them so far. Nuclear terrorism would be both technically and logistically difficult to achieve (Melley 2017), which is another reason it's less likely that this would happen.

Right now, there are nine countries that possess nuclear weapons: the United States, the United Kingdom, Russia, France, India, Pakistan, China, Israel, and North Korea (Kristensen et al. 2024), but any industrialized country that has a nuclear power plant (such as Japan, Brazil, or South Korea) could create one within a few months if it chose to (U.N. 2023). Right now, 88% of all nuclear weapons in the world are held by Russia and the US (Kristensen et al. 2024), and the risk of them being used is higher than it has been at any time since the Cold War (U.N. 2023).

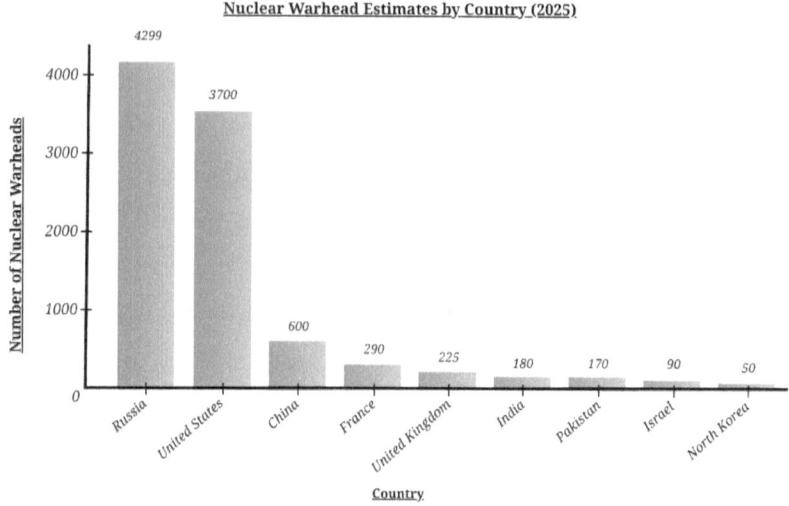

We've seen in the news over recent years the extent of the tensions between the most powerful countries in the world, and nuclear modernization programs have been a part of this. Besides Russia's threats to Ukraine, we've seen that the US and China are very close to having a nuclear arms race, and the development of nuclear weapons in North Korea continues to advance (Mecklin 2024). In addition, the risk of any of these weapons being used is increased by emerging technologies, and we have a clear reason to be concerned. Cyber attacks have already caused a great deal of harm and disruption over recent years—what would happen if they were used to manipulate the information given to decision-makers who have the power to launch nuclear weapons? Machine learning, meanwhile, is increasingly being used in defense systems, and this could give decision-makers a much smaller window of time in which to decide whether a nuclear weapon will be launched. Any nuclear weapon could potentially be compromised or hacked using technology, so in an already volatile situation, this could make the risk much greater (ICAN n.d.).

NUCLEAR POWER

It was the thought of nuclear weapons that led to me thinking about nuclear power, and, honestly, this scares me much less. However, it does come with hazards, and there's still a risk of a serious accident happening as a result of nuclear energy programs. We'll look at some of the most significant incidents from the past to illustrate this, but first, let's think about how great our risk is.

There are currently around 440 nuclear reactors in operation across the world, which, in 2023, produced around 9% of our global electricity. On top of this, more countries are considering the idea of beginning nuclear power programs, and many already have plans to build further reactors (World Nuclear Association 2025). In 2024, the US had 94 nuclear reactors spread across 28 states (US Energy Information Administration 2024). The Nuclear Regulatory Commission outlines two risk zones for anyone living near a nuclear power plant. If you live within 10 miles of one, an incident could mean that you're exposed to radiation, which would put you at the greatest risk. If you live within 50 miles of one, there's a risk that an incident could contaminate food and water supplies, and recommendations are now that if an accident were to occur, the evacuation zone would span this radius (Stromberg 2014). In North Carolina, for example, there are four nuclear power plants, and

16 | WHAT ARE WE WORRYING ABOUT? THE POTENTIAL DANGER...

both zones are included in the emergency planning for a potential accident in the state (ReadyNC.gov n.d.).

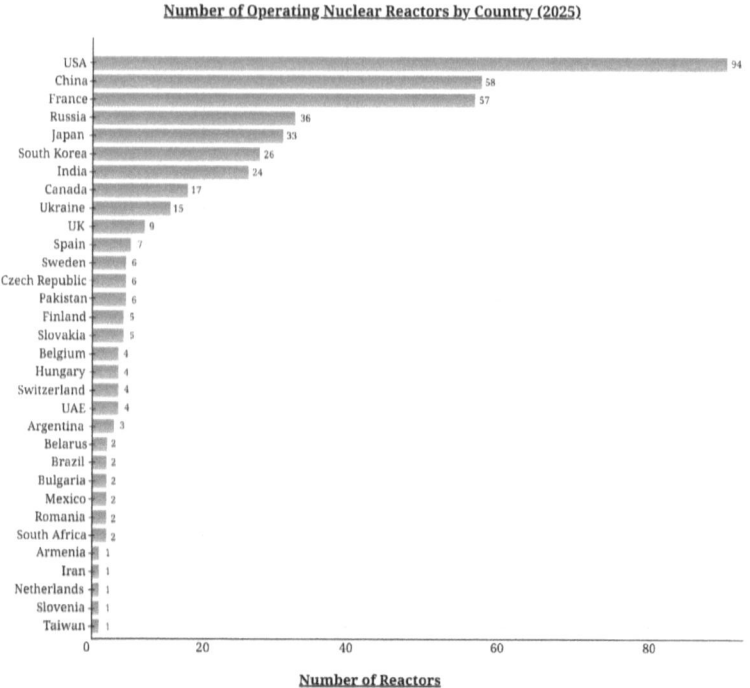

In Oklahoma, where I live, there are no nuclear reactors, for which I'm very grateful. Kate, my wife, is from Australia, and we go back to visit family occasionally. I'm happy to say there are none there, too—not across the whole country. Their government is concerned that it would risk their energy security, raise their expenses, risk the health of both the community and the environment, and use more water than the country can afford to gamble with (Climate Council 2025). Much of the US, however, is more at risk, and at the end of the chapter, we'll look at how you can assess your region. First, though, let's take a brief look back through history at the accidents that both show us that there's reason for concern and have helped to make the current state of nuclear power much safer.

The most recent devastating accident happened on the northeast coast of Japan in 2011 at the Fukushima Dai-ichi nuclear power plant. It started with an earthquake, which cut off the external power to the reactors. A tsunami, which reached much greater heights than the plant was designed to accommodate, then disabled the backup generators, preventing the reactor cooling systems from doing their job. Fuel overheated in the reactor cores, and this led to huge hydrogen explosions and the release of a dangerous amount of radiation. As a result, almost half a million local residents were forced to evacuate (Union of Concerned Scientists 2013).

Twenty-five years earlier, in 1986, there was an accident in Ukraine, which is widely considered to be the worst nuclear disaster the world has ever seen. This was at Chornobyl, where a sudden power surge during a test on the reactor systems caused an explosion that destroyed an entire unit of the plant. A large amount of radiation escaped, and around 220,000 local residents were forced to evacuate (Union of Concerned Scientists 2013).

There have been a number of other accidents at nuclear power plants, spanning the years between 1952 when there was a meltdown at the Chalk River facility near Ottawa in Canada, and 2019, when there was a radiation accident at the State Navy Testing Range at Nyonoksa in Russia, but none so devastating as these two infamous ones (atomicarchive.com n.d.).

Each one has helped specialists and operators refine their systems and improve safety measures, which lessens our risk today. However, this is nuclear energy: We should never assume that nothing could go wrong. Plus, if there were to be an attack on any of them, such as the one threatened by Putin, the risk would become much greater.

TAKE ACTION!

As you may recall, there are close to 440 operational nuclear reactors around the world. You don't know what the chances of an incident with any of these are, but what you can do is find out if you live near any of them. Find out whether there's a nuclear power plant in your region, and work out how far away you are from the ones closest to you (looking up The World Nuclear Association is a good place to start). This will tell you more about your risk if something were to happen there. If you look online, you'll find maps of operating commercial power stations in the US, and you'll also find the emergency advice given within those states. It was doing this exercise that allowed me to confirm that I don't live near one; if you do, you'll need to bear this in mind as you make your preparations and consider your risk.

The next question, then, is, what are those risks? What dangers does nuclear energy present, and what do you need to be aware of if any of these things happen? This is what we'll explore in the next chapter.

2

AND THEN WHAT? THE EFFECTS OF NUCLEAR FALLOUT AND RADIATION

In Chapter 5, we're going to look at how to talk to your family about the possibility of a nuclear disaster, but I have to admit, my kids made it easy for me. They're huge fans of *The Simpsons*, and if you've ever watched more than a few episodes, you're bound to have come across the bright green sludgy liquid indicating nuclear waste. For the uninitiated, the show takes place in the fictional town of Springfield, which has a nuclear power plant, and radioactive waste often makes an ominous appearance on the show. After seeing this many, many times, my kids finally asked me about what nuclear energy actually is, and I found myself thinking about the depiction of it in *The Simpsons*, wondering if this undermines how serious it would be if there really was nuclear waste lurking around every corner.

THE TRUTH ABOUT NUCLEAR WASTE

The Simpsons has it right: Nuclear energy produces radioactive waste. The difference is that it's not oozing green sludge, and it's much more dangerous. It can fall into two broad categories: high-level and low-level waste. High-level waste is most commonly fuel removed from reactors once electricity has been produced; low-level waste comes from any other use of radioactive materials (such as in research or in the daily operations involving nuclear reactors). High-level waste is generally uranium, which is no longer efficient enough to produce electricity. It's very hot, highly radioactive, and needs to be handled remotely; what's more, as of 2022, the US had over 90,000 tons of it to dispose of (Ghosh 2022). When fission occurs, the uranium atoms split, which creates the energy used to make electricity, as well as resulting in radioactive isotopes known as "fission products." These are what cause much of the heat and radiation that comes from high-level waste. During the fission process, some atoms of uranium pick up neutrons and form heavier elements, which, while not producing as much heat or radiation, take a long time to decay. This is known as "transuranic waste," and it can continue to be a radioactive hazard thousands of years after it's created. High-level waste produces fatal doses of radiation if we're exposed to it for even a short period, and if it gets into a river or groundwater, it could enter the food chain, resulting in indirect exposure (United States Nuclear Regulatory Commission, 2024).

Nuclear waste goes through a process of radioactive decay, decreasing the level of threat it poses, but this happens over time. It's also true that most of the waste produced by the nuclear power industry doesn't have a high level of radioactivity, and protections are in place to make sure that it doesn't get into the outside environment (although the production of nuclear weapons does also result in high-level waste (Ghosh 2022)). The concern is, what happens if something goes wrong?

What Could Go Wrong?

Although there are regulations to ensure the safety of nuclear operations, there are still unpredictable dangers like natural hazards, equipment failure, and human error. If there were to be a severe accident like a meltdown in a reactor, radiation could leak into the environment. Should an explosion occur, this would likely result in nuclear fallout (meaning that radioactive debris could be launched into the outside environment). These concerns grow as climate change unfolds. Nuclear power plants are very vulnerable to changes in water and air temperature, and they don't do well with extreme weather; these factors can compromise the reactors and increase safety risks. Even now, some power plants have received permission from the Nuclear Regulatory Committee to raise the maximum temperature for the water they let back into the environment, which could have a negative impact on water quality (Ghosh 2022). Essentially, the safety of nuclear power plants is in jeopardy because of the effects of climate change, and this could have devastating effects on both public health and the environment at large. In the event of an emergency, it would be workers and emergency responders who would have the highest risk of radiation exposure at first, but it's also possible that the radioactive risk could spread to a wider area.

The Health Risks of Radiation

Radiation has its uses as a medical tool, but it's important not to mix this up with the serious effects of high doses of radiation. When it's used in a medical setting (such as when you have an X-ray), there's some risk involved, but doses are low enough that the benefits are considered to outweigh the costs (Newman 2023). The radiation you may be exposed to after a nuclear accident, however, would not be so controlled.

There are a few different types of ionizing radiation (which simply means radiation with so much energy that it can remove an electron from an atom), the main three being alpha particles, beta particles, and gamma rays. Alpha particles only become a health issue if they're inhaled or ingested, when they can damage both your cells and your DNA, increasing your risk of cancer. Beta particles have more energy but are much smaller than alpha particles, and this means they can travel further. Because they're small, however, they have less ionizing power and are less likely to cause damage to the human body. Gamma rays are often emitted during radioactive decay, and we're very vulnerable to these. Indeed, they're the main hazard for anyone who has to handle radioactive materials. When we're dealing with nuclear power plants and weapons, we also have to consider neutrons, which are the uncharged particles released during the nuclear fission process. These can be very harmful and destructive to human tissue, but they have the power to make a previously safe material radioactive (World Nuclear Association 2024).

In whichever form it takes, ionizing radiation is a serious health risk if we're exposed to high doses of it. Very high doses could result in radiation sickness and death. Even in low doses, it can cause cardiovascular disease and cancer, and children and teenagers are particularly vulnerable to this because their bodies haven't yet finished developing (National Cancer Institute n.d.). An accident at a nuclear power plant (which would release iodine-131, among other radioactive isotopes) could expose us to ionizing radiation through contaminated air or, indirectly, through contaminated food or water. I mention iodine-131 specifically because this affects the thyroid gland, which controls how quickly your body is able to use energy. It uses iodine to produce hormones for this process, but it can't distinguish between non-radioactive iodine and iodine-131; therefore, exposure to this radioactive isotope can increase your risk of thyroid cancer for a long time after the event (National Cancer Institute n.d.).

We're at risk of other radioactive isotopes, too, if, for example, we walk on earth that's been contaminated or breathe in contaminated air, and this can affect any organ or tissue in the body.

The main reason researchers understand the risks associated with radiation exposure comes, ironically, from previous accidents at nuclear power plants. In particular, a lot of research was conducted after Chornobyl, when many power plant workers who were on-site at the time developed radiation sickness. Those who had been exposed to very high doses died; some of those who had a lower exposure survived. People who were involved in the cleanup afterward were found to be more at risk of developing leukemia, while residents of the surrounding area were more at risk of thyroid cancer (National Cancer Institute n.d.).

Radioactive Fallout

When there's a nuclear explosion, radioactive particles fall to the ground. It depends on the nature of the explosion, which is exactly what this consists of, but it could involve fission products, radioactive soil, or weapon debris, and the particles could vary in size. Most of this debris will fall close to where the explosion happened, but some of it will get high in the atmosphere, which means it will be spread much further. Within the first 24 hours of an explosion, this is referred to as "early fallout," but "delayed fallout" could happen days, weeks, months, or even years after the event (atomicarchive.com n.d.).

Discussing the science behind the TV show "Fallout," Professor Pran Nath of Northeastern University said that if a nuclear device were to be dropped, we would see three stages of devastation. In the first, the nuclear reaction would create gamma rays, resulting in a large and highly destructive flash. In the second phase, we'd see a blast of heat and a shockwave containing so much pressure that it could destroy concrete buildings. The final phase is the fallout, which lasts for longer and has wide-ranging effects. "These radioactive elements," he said, "have lifetimes which could be a few seconds and could be up to millions of years … It causes pollution and damage to the body and injuries over a longer period, causing cancer and leukemia …" (Mello-Klein 2024).

THREE PHASES OF NUCLEAR EXPLOSION

	FIRST PHASE	Gamma rays, large destructive flash
	SECOND PHASE	Heat and shockwave, destruction of buildings
	FINAL PHASE	Fallout, radiation, long-term effects

Alarmingly, a weapon doesn't even have to be activated for this to happen. Fallout also occurs when nuclear weapons are tested. When they're tested above ground, radioactive materials are sent high into the atmosphere (up to 50 miles sometimes). The large particles fall close to the explosion, but lighter ones, as well as gases, go much higher and could circulate through the atmosphere before they eventually fall where the wind takes them (United States Environmental Protection Agency n.d.). Thankfully, the Comprehensive Nuclear-Test-Ban Treaty, which was signed in 1996, has put an end to most overground testing, although The Democratic People's Republic of Korea conducted a test like this as recently as 2017 (United Nations n.d.).

It's important to remember, though, that fallout is not only the result of nuclear weapons: An explosion at a power plant would have the same effect. Indeed, the lighter particles of fallout from Chornobyl didn't just fall over Ukraine; the wind also took them to Russia, Belarus, and some further parts of Europe and Scandinavia, which resulted in social, economic, and health consequences in these areas (World Nuclear Association n.d.).

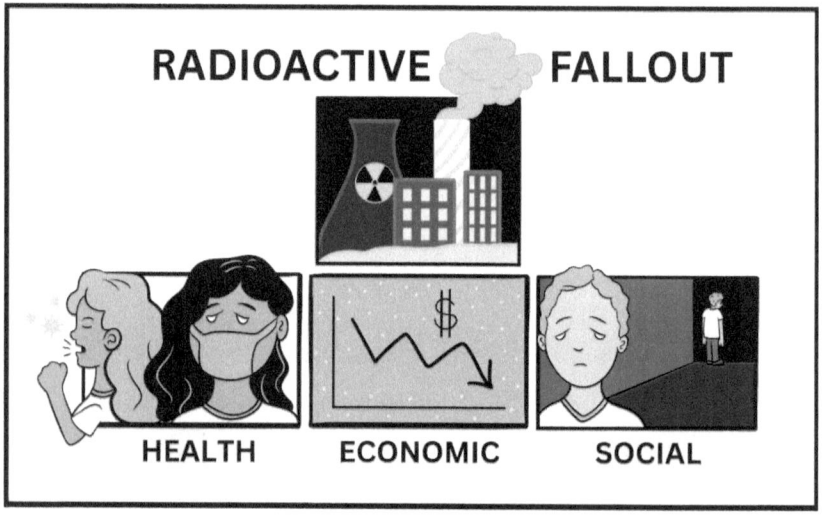

THE IMPACT OF A NUCLEAR ATTACK

I'm going to make a distinction here between a nuclear attack and nuclear war because although nuclear weapons are at the center of both of them, the effects would be very different. When I'm talking about a nuclear attack, I'm referring to an attack in which a device is used to create a nuclear explosion. It's possible that an attack like this could be carried out by a government, but it could also be done by a terrorist group, in which case, it might involve an improvised nuclear device

(IND)—which is to say that it may be built crudely using parts of stolen weapons or built from scratch. This isn't easy to do (even obtaining parts of nuclear weapons), so it's unlikely, but we should be aware that it's a possibility.

Based on analysis from the US Department of Homeland Security, if an attack like this were to take place, there could be serious injuries and fatalities, and areas of cities could be destroyed. The fallout, as we saw in the last section, could affect the local population for years to come, and there could be massive disruptions to infrastructure. The spread of damage would depend on the size of the nuclear device and the geography of the area. Again, the fallout could potentially travel miles away from the site of the explosion, affecting areas further afield. Closer to this, if the device were to produce an electromagnetic pulse (EMP), it could disrupt electronic equipment and destroy vital parts of the local infrastructure.

The level of fatality from an attack like this would be would depend on how many people were nearby, the size of the device, and what the weather conditions were like at the time. There would likely be injuries from the shockwave and severe burns caused by the thermal energy from the explosion. Survivors of the explosion may suffer consequences to their health as a result of radiation, which could include short-term effects like Acute Radiation Syndrome (ARS) and skin burns or may later reveal long-term consequences like an increased risk for cancer. For those exposed to high levels of radiation, the central nervous system could become compromised, resulting in death, and the fetuses of pregnant women who are exposed may be born with impaired brain function or malformations (US Department of Homeland Security).

THE IMPACT OF A NUCLEAR WAR

A single nuclear attack could have devastating consequences, but it all gets a little more scary when we're thinking about an all-out nuclear war. Let's start small, though: A nuclear war, after all, would begin with a bomb, from which we'd see similar effects to those of an isolated nuclear attack. However, we're now talking about expertly manufactured weapons, and direct radiation is likely to be less significant than the other lethal effects. There is, however, an exception. The enhanced-radiation weapon, otherwise known as the neutron bomb, is designed to minimize other destructive effects while maximizing its radiation (Wolfson and Dalnoki-Veress 2022).

A nuclear weapon is solid and cold before it explodes, but after just microseconds, it will become hotter than the sun's core, radiating X-rays into the surrounding air. The extreme temperature of the air will cause a fireball to form, which will grow in diameter, glow brightly, and radiate a deadly amount of heat. This is known as a "thermal flash," and it can start fires and burn us severely, even 20 miles away from the explosion. As the thermal flash puts pressure on the air around it, a blast wave (a sudden rise in air pressure) occurs, moving outwards and carrying a lot of the weapon's explosive energy with it. This is what causes the majority of the physical damage to the area, and its effects can cause many additional fatalities. If the explosion happens in the air (an air burst), the blast wave will reflect off the ground, and this will increase the level of destruction it causes. If it happens on the ground (a ground burst), the blast is likely not to reach as far. A ground burst is more likely to be used to hit a military target, but if there's to be a nuclear attack on a city, it would be more likely for air bursts to be used (Wolfson and Dalnoki-Veress 2022).

The actual explosion wouldn't last for very long. Even the blast wave would be over in a matter of minutes—but this doesn't mean its effects would. Fire would spread, perhaps even developing into a firestorm, and, of course, there would still be fallout. As we've seen, this could last for many years, but the most immediate lethal effects would be over much more quickly, and as you'll see later in the book, the recommendations are that survivors should shelter indoors for at least 48 hours. We're looking at something slightly different with the fallout from a nuclear weapon than we were with a nuclear power plant, though. A weapon like this is packed with a large amount of radioactive material, and the cloud it creates can rise very high; this means that lethal fallout could travel over hundreds of miles, depending on the weather conditions. The only good news here is that the fallout will become less deadly quite quickly because of radioactive decay (Wolfson and Dalnoki-Veress 2022).

Again, we have to talk about electromagnetic pulse. If the explosion were to take place at a high altitude, it could affect an area covering hundreds of miles, creating an EMP strong enough to damage satellites, communication systems, computers, and a range of other electronic devices (Wolfson and Dalnoki-Veress 2022).

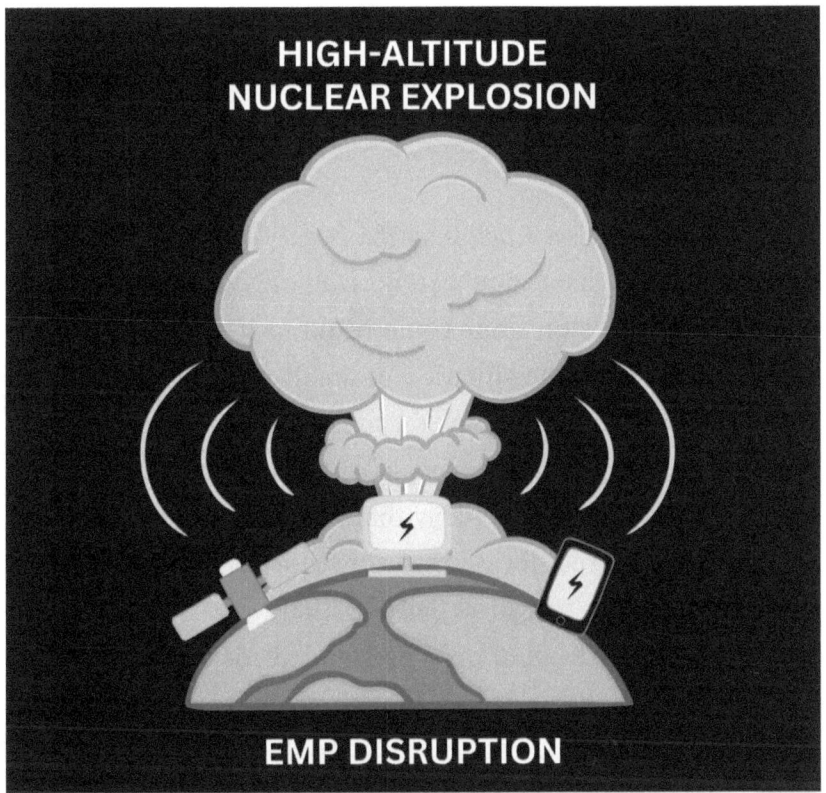

We also have to consider the environmental damage of a nuclear blast. The International Red Cross has conducted research that concluded that even in a limited nuclear war, around 5 million tons of soot could be produced by the fires, and this would cause the global temperature to fall by around 34.34°F. This would, in turn, affect food production, and we would be facing widespread starvation (Campaign for Nuclear Disarmament n.d.).

This is all alarming enough, but we've been talking about a single nuclear explosion. An all-out nuclear war would involve many more explosions than this, and in all honesty, we have no experience to inform us of exactly how devastating that would be. A great many people would be killed across a large area, and for survivors in lesser affected places, the consequences are still likely to be dire.

In their book, *Nuclear Choices for the Twenty-First Century*, scientists Richard Wolfson and Ferenc Dalnoki-Veress reflect that one nuclear explosion alone could result in 10,000 cases of very severe burns, so in the situation of an all-out war, the number of similar cases could be several million. They raise the question of what care would be available to help people who were injured—it would be very likely that hospitals and medical staff would have suffered devastating consequences, too. In a situation like this, the spread of lethal fallout would be vast, and radiation exposure could only be avoided for those who were able to retain shelter and had enough water, food, and medical supplies to see them through. What would happen after this is, to an extent, impossible to predict, but we could expect the spread of disease (due to contaminated food and water, the lack of medical care, and the loss of sanitary facilities), inadequate access to necessary supplies, and a breakdown of infrastructure. To survive in these circumstances, we would need to work hard, and we'd need to work together. We would all have suffered great loss and, in all likelihood, watched people we care about suffer. We would need to rebuild society, and it may look very different from what we're currently familiar with—and we'd need to do it after considerable damage to the environment (Wolfson and Dalnoki-Veress 2022).

You may have heard of the idea of a nuclear winter. This is a theory about what would happen to the climate following a nuclear war, and researchers predict that the smoke from the fires would heat in the sun and spread across the globe through the upper stratosphere, resulting in a cooler, darker, drier climate. For at least one year, we wouldn't be able to grow crops, and this would mean that many people would starve. The ozone would be very damaged in this situation, and this would mean that we would be exposed to a large level of ultraviolet radiation from the sun (John Wiley & Sons, Ltd. 2010). Researchers propose that these devastating climatic conditions would lead to fatalities and starvation across the globe (Toon et al. 2019).

When I was researching this book, I hesitated about whether to include these devastating potential effects of nuclear war because the reality is that this is something we can do very little to prepare for. However, in the end, I felt like leaving it out would have been to sugarcoat the issue, and I believe that a big part of being prepared is having knowledge—even if you can't physically prepare for a particular outcome. We won't focus on this too much from here on because the survival chances of our entire species would hang in the balance, and this isn't something it makes sense to focus our energies on as we try to become as prepared as we possibly can be.

PHYSICAL HEALTH ISN'T OUR ONLY CONCERN

There is one more thing I'd like to draw your attention to before we move forward, though. No matter what the nature of a nuclear emergency, we're not only preparing for physical risk; we're also preparing for the toll it's going to take on our emotional and psychological health. This would be at its most extreme in the case of an all-out nuclear war, and just as an important part of preparation is awareness of the physical risks, being aware of the psychological impact is advisable.

An accident at a nuclear power plant is likely to come with psychological risk, too. A significant disaster of any kind can trigger symptoms of posttraumatic stress, depression, and anxiety in those affected by it (Goldman and Galea 2013), and a nuclear disaster is no exception. Indeed, many experts regard the mental health ramifications of Chornobyl to be the greatest health problem caused by the accident (Bromet and Havenaar 2007), and after the accident at Fukushima, more mental health problems arose because of the nuclear disaster than because of the natural disaster that caused it (Maeda, Oe, and Suzuki 201). Researchers believe that the emotional consequences of nuclear disasters like this relate not only to the trauma of the incident but also to the fear of developing cancer as a result. The groups most at risk are those involved in the clean-up after an accident and the mothers of young children (Bromet 2015), but anyone could be affected.

TAKE ACTION!

I have no desire to instill fear in you, but it's good to be aware of the potential dangers that lie ahead. Take this mini-quiz to test your knowledge of previous nuclear disasters and shake off the heavy feeling before we move into active preparation. You'll find the answers at the end of the book.

1. What was the main reason for the Chornobyl accident?
2. Which natural disaster led to the nuclear disaster at Fukushima?
3. What is nuclear fission?
4. What is the name of the treaty preventing nuclear weapons testing?
5. When was the most recent serious nuclear power plant disaster?

It's important to understand what we're preparing for, and the next part of our journey is to make sure that we're as ready as possible. The most important part of this, at least in the immediate aftermath of a nuclear disaster, is shelter, which is what we'll look at in the next chapter.

3

STAYING SAFE ... AS FAR INSIDE AS YOU CAN GET

Shelter is a fundamental part of survival, but it becomes even more important in the face of a nuclear disaster. Should there be a nuclear accident of any kind, your first priority should be to find shelter—or to stay inside if you are already indoors.

SHELTER OR EVACUATE?

One of the questions that gets asked a lot when it comes to nuclear survival is whether people should shelter or evacuate. The answer is both: First, we shelter; *then,* we evacuate.

You might be inclined to get away as quickly as possible, but even if you have the minimal shelter a car will provide, it won't be enough to protect you from radiation as you make your way to your destination. Radiation levels are at their most dangerous in the immediate aftermath of a nuclear incident, and the safest time to leave is after a few days when they reduce. The less time you're exposed, the lower the health risks, and this means having the densest materials possible between you and the source and getting as far inside as you can. If you're at home when the blast happens, the best thing you can do is go to a room in the center of the building or into a basement with no windows or doors. Close up all the doors and windows, and shut off any air conditioning or heating units that bring in air from outside to reduce the risk of fallout coming inside. It would also be a good idea to seal doors and air vents—essentially, you want to close off as much air from the outside as possible. If you're not at home, you want to get into a concrete or brick building as quickly as you can. If you're stuck in your car and there's no way to get to a building safely, you'll have a small amount of protection, but make sure you close all the vents and windows (Monmouth County, N.J. n.d.).

If we find ourselves in this situation, emergency responders and local authorities will work together to tell you when it's safe to evacuate; don't leave your shelter until they let you know it's time. I know this would make me extremely anxious if my kids weren't home, but I also know that the safest thing to do would be to leave them where they are. If your children are in school or at childcare, it would be best for them to stay there and go as far inside the building as possible. The staff taking care of them will be in the same position, and they'll do their best to protect them; trying to get them out before evacuation is safe will only serve to put both of you in danger.

FINDING SUITABLE SHELTER

Researchers from the University of Nicosia in Cyprus have shown that the best place to shelter in the event of a nuclear blast is in a sturdy building, ideally in a corner and as far away as possible from any windows or doors. Using computer modeling, they looked at how a 750-kiloton nuclear blast wave would move through a building, taking into account the strong wind speeds that would accompany it. They concluded that the most dangerous place to be would be by windows or doors or in corridors (where the wind speeds pick up) and that the corner of the room would be the safest place (because the highest winds would be likely to miss these). The ideal spot within the home would be in the corner of an internal room, like a closet. They also emphasized, however, that this would only be successful if the building was strong enough to survive the blast in the first place (Brahambhatt 2023).

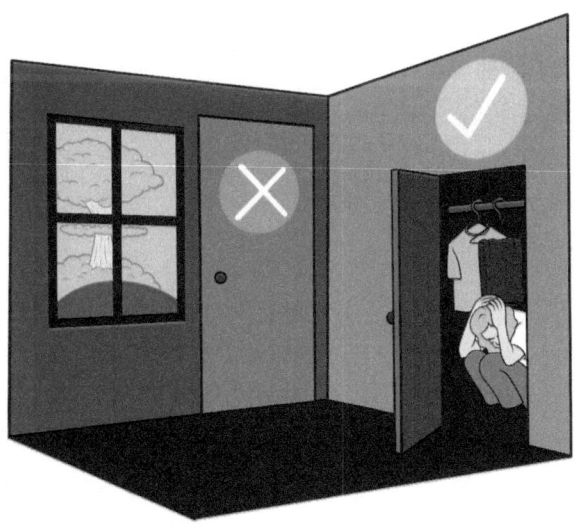

If you live in a city, the safest place is an underground space. Ideally, this would be a purpose-built fallout shelter, but even a subway or a basement would provide more protection than a structure raised above ground level. Better yet, and only possible if you live outside the city, would be in the countryside surrounded by hills, where the natural landscape would provide more shelter from the blast, although this would not protect you from radiation carried by the wind and isn't a possibility if you live in the city (Thomson 2023).

If your home is not made of concrete or brick or it only has one or two stories, your best bet is to stay in the middle, as far away as possible from the outer walls and roof. If there's no basement for you to shelter in, the best place is the first floor or the middle floor. In a multi-story building, your safest spot will be the basement or parking levels (US Department of Homeland Security 2021).

I'd recommend scouting for possible shelter locations near every place where you have to spend a lot of time—so at home or near your place of work. Remember that you may not be at home at the time of a blast, so it would be prudent to find a potential shelter everywhere you regularly visit, particularly keeping an eye out for buildings with basements or underground parking lots.

FALLOUT SHELTERS

The best possible protection in the event of a nuclear disaster is a fallout shelter or nuclear bunker, which will provide both physical protection and protection from radioactive debris. A shelter like this is an enclosed space built with thick shielding designed to reduce your exposure to gamma rays. This is made out of concrete, lead, packed earth, or a combination of the three. It's possible to have a shelter like this in your home, but, in the opinion of Subterranean Spaces, who design shelters like this, it's better (and less costly) to build them underground. This offers added protection to the earth around it and is less of a drain on space. Fallout shelters are equipped with blast doors, which are designed to absorb the impact of a blast and shield you from the shockwaves. They're also designed to be habitable, so they're built with internal air cooling systems and are appropriate for a specified number of people to shelter in for at least two weeks without needing to leave, which means stocking them with water and food and ensuring sanitation (Subterranean Spaces n.d.).

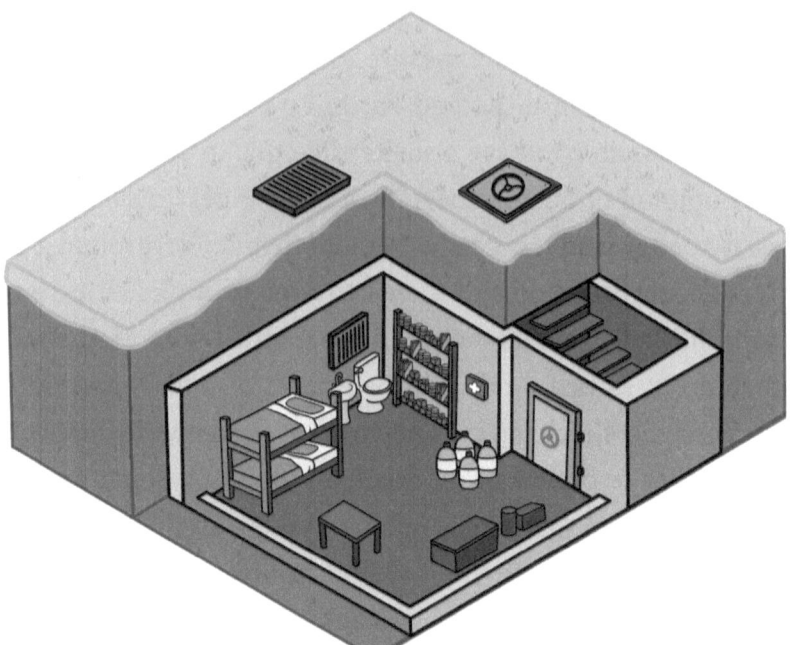

If you can afford one of these, the ideal place for it would be in an open space away from your property, and it should be built lower than a regular storage bunker would be. You want enough earth on top of it to protect you from the radiation, and you'll need a sealed door, as well as a generator to give you power for a couple of weeks. Your shelter should also have an integrated air system that will filter the air and protect you from radiation, as well as sanitation facilities and plenty of storage for your provisions (Subterranean Spaces n.d.). If you don't have the space outside your property, you could also consider turning your basement, if you have one, into a panic room—something that companies like this are also able to install.

If you search online, you'll also find a range of different styles of one-off purpose-built shelters available to buy. These range in price from about $20,000 to $250,000 and are often already set in a specific location, which may not be anywhere that's of practical use to you in an unanticipated emergency.

Of course, a purpose-built fallout shelter isn't a realistic option for everyone, but this doesn't mean you can't learn from its principles. Something that's definitely manageable is planning a fallout room within your home, within which you can then create an inner refuge. This is something the Central Office of Information advised in the late 1970s, but its guidance is still useful today.

Bear in mind that in order to protect yourself from radiation, you may need to stay in this room for two weeks, so it will need to be well-equipped (we'll discuss how you can do this a little later). Remember, you want to choose a room as far away from the outside walls and roof as possible, ideally a basement. All openings, including the windows, will need to be blocked, and it would be a good idea to make any outside walls you do have (as well as the floor above you) as thick as you can using dense materials like concrete, bricks, sand, timber, boxes of earth, or even books. The danger of radiation exposure will be at its highest in the first couple of days, so you'll want to have an inner refuge within your fallout room to protect you from this. Again, you want to make sure that this is lined with dense materials, keeping it as far from the outside walls as you can. You could do this by creating a lean-to using strong boards and an interior wall (make sure to fix wood to the floor, too, so the boards don't slip). Around the outside of your refuge, you can add an extra layer of protection by covering it with sand, earth, books, or any other dense material. The two open ends can then be closed with heavy furniture or boxes of sand or earth. Alternatively, you could use a large table surrounded by and covered with dense materials (The Central Office of Information 1976).

Building Your Own Shelter

If you have the space, which I acknowledge you may not, you could also consider building your own shelter. Your protection may not be as good as it would be with a purpose-built shelter, but it will still be a lot better than having no shelter at all. If you do this in your backyard, it should be at least half the height of the house closest to it and away from large trees so that you minimize the risk of it being compromised if things collapse in an explosion. You will need to consult local regulations before attempting to build something like this, and you may need to apply for permission.

One option you have is to improvise a shelter using materials you already have around your house. Start by choosing a space where the ground is level and rainwater is unlikely to collect. You'll then need to dig a trench around three feet wide, five feet deep, and 11 feet long. If you plan to accommodate more than four people, you'll need to add an extra three feet to the length for each extra person (Barnes 2023). Now, dig an entrance that slopes down into the shelter and a ventilation trench just beneath the surface of the ground at the other end. This will need to have an opening at the far end in order to allow the air to circulate, but make sure that the trench is no shorter than five feet so that this opening isn't too close to the shelter. Then, line your shelter with heavy-duty polythene sheeting, followed by timber, which you'll need to fortify with dense materials like carpets and blankets. You'll need to make sure your shelter has doors and that it is covered with a minimum of 18 inches of earth (Central Office of Information 1981). Create a barrier using sandbags a couple of feet away from the entrance to increase your protection in this area. You can make sandbags yourself using sand packed into pillowcases or plastic sacks.

If you don't have the necessary materials already, you can use DIY materials to build your shelter. Scaffolding poles used to create A-frames over your trench would be an asset here. Again, line your trench with heavy-duty polythene sheeting and top this with timber before constructing the frame with your scaffolding poles (wood will also work). Cover this structure with plywood boards, sealing any gaps between them with thick fabric or carpet. You can then wrap the whole structure in heavy-duty polythene, making sure that the pieces overlap so that there are no gaps. Top this with something dense like a mattress or a layer of straw, and, again, cover your shelter with at least 18 inches of earth. This DIY version is more sealed, which will offer better protection, but this means you'll also have to make sure that it has adequate ventilation. You could use metal drainpipes for this, but make sure the opening faces downwards and is packed with steel wool to provide a filter.

You can also buy manufactured kits that you can install inside your home. These are generally made of steel and will protect you from the debris if your home collapses in the blast, but they tend to be more like tables, so you'd have to surround one of these with sandbags, heavy furniture, or another dense material to protect you from the fallout. There are kits designed for outdoor use, too, which is more likely to be a sealed room. These should be sunk into the ground and covered over with earth (Central Office of Information 1981).

I'll admit that I haven't done any of this myself yet, although I will do this in the future. My wife and I are currently weighing how concerned we are about a nuclear threat, and at this stage, we've concluded that it's wise to have some kind of a plan in place, but we haven't yet gone so far as to build a shelter. It is in our future, but I do want to reassure you that you have options, and if this isn't possible for you, you can still make plans about where to go when you have to shelter without having a purpose-built structure.

WHERE TO GO AFTER THE FALLOUT

What we've done so far, at least in terms of shelter preparation, is find the safest place in our home and turn it into a fallout room, just as I described earlier. We've also scoped out the safest buildings to use if something happened to our home or we weren't there at the time of the blast. The best buildings to take shelter in this situation are those that are reinforced with concrete, as they're less likely to collapse. It's thought that it would be best to avoid the top two stories of any building higher than five floors, remembering that the basement is your safest option (Newkey-Burden 2024). I raise this again because once you've been given the all-clear to evacuate, you need somewhere to go. It's likely that your local authority will have a plan in place for this, but in my opinion, it's best to have your own plan in case this isn't how it turns out.

TAKE ACTION!

Assess the safest place in your house for your family to shelter if it becomes necessary, and make sure everyone knows where it is. On your commute or when you're out and about in daily life, identify nearby buildings or subways that may serve you better once you've been given the all-clear to evacuate.

Shelter is your immediate concern in the event of a nuclear disaster, but it isn't the only thing you need to worry about. In the next chapter, we'll look at what else you need to consider and how best to prepare for it.

4

BE PREPARED! WHAT YOU CAN DO TO GET READY NOW

It depends on how extensive your preparations for other emergencies are as to how much extra you'll need to do to prepare for a nuclear disaster. If you've read my previous books, you'll find that a lot of the guidance within them will help you prepare your stocks to see you through a nuclear disaster. Radiation and fallout aside, the basic principles of survival remain the same: You need to be able to survive without access to the things we usually take for granted. You'll find details about different aspects of this in my other books, but in case you haven't read them yet, in this chapter, you'll find a brief overview of what you'll need.

We'll also, of course, offer advice specific to a nuclear disaster, so even if you do have your stocks in place, keep reading. There are some crucial additions you'll need to make in order to survive a nuclear disaster.

WHAT SHOULD BE INSIDE YOUR SHELTER

Firstly, I want to be clear that in this chapter, when I'm talking about stocking your shelter, I mean the space in which you'll take refuge in the event of a nuclear emergency—it doesn't matter if this is a purpose-built shelter or a fallout room you've created within your home.

Before we get into the stocks you'll need inside whatever space it is you'll be using to protect yourself, I want to start with the most important thing you need to get in place before you start moving supplies into a purpose-built shelter, and that's ventilation.

Ventilation

It's no good protecting yourself from a nuclear disaster only to run out of oxygen a day in. If you build a shelter, you'll also need to make sure you install a ventilation system that will last for several months and be able to survive the blast. You're going to be trying to close off much of the outside air, and that means that you need to think about the air on the inside, which will mean filtering it to remove contaminants. Without something like this, you run the risk of dangerously high levels of carbon dioxide, especially if you have several people using the shelter. The water vapor and heat alone could be fatal in this situation (Kearny 2004). Installing a carbon dioxide scrubber, which you can find easily online, will reduce this risk (Alfaintek n.d.).

Water

The difference here from prepping for other types of disaster is that rainwater harvesting and filling bathtubs up with water as soon as you hear of an incident aren't an option. All of these water sources could be contaminated, and the only way you can be sure to have access to safe drinking water is to stockpile it in advance.

I'd advise stocking up on enough drinking water for your family for two weeks. You'll need at least a gallon per person per day to allow this, but if you can stock more, do (US Department of Homeland Security n.d.). You'll also need water for washing because it's unlikely that you'll be able to use the water supply in your home. Keep all of your water in sealed containers: Any water that contains fallout debris will be contaminated, and this isn't something you can solve by boiling it (CDC 2024).

The easiest option is to store a supply of bottled water (check that it's appropriate for long-term storage first, though), keeping it in a cool, dark spot out of direct sunlight. Remember, too, to check the expiration dates regularly and rotate your supplies. Alternatively, you could use tap water, but you'll need to make sure it's stored in food-grade containers or barrels designed especially for long-term water storage. Again, keep your containers somewhere cool and dark, and make sure they're well sealed. It may be tap water this time, but you'll still need to rotate your stocks, so keep the date on each container and switch them out every six months (Baumgart 2024).

Food

When it comes to food, if you're prepared for a natural disaster, you have what you need to feed your family in the event of a nuclear one. The only thing you won't have access to is your garden; anything you've preserved and any non-perishables that you've stocked up on, provided they're in sealed containers, will be safe to use.

Again, you want to stock enough to cover you for at least two weeks. You'll need to keep a healthy stock of canned and dried foods that you can cook within your shelter. Good items to consider are wheat, rice, beans, honey, sugar, pasta, oats, dried vegetables and fruits, and powdered milk, but I'll refer you to *The Prepper's Pantry* for more details on stocking a healthy pantry with a long shelf life. What I will say, though, is that it would be wise to stock a lot of calorie-dense foods to make sure everyone keeps their energy levels up.

Tools

I don't need to tell you that things break. You don't want to be stuck in your shelter with a broken bed or appliance. You need a way to fix anything that needs mending. If you're anything like me, though, you've probably acquired enough tools to fill a garden shed, and you obviously don't want all of those down there with you. You might want to consider investing in a survival multi-tool that contains pliers, blades, screwdrivers, and other helpful items in a single piece of equipment. Alternatively, build yourself a survival toolbox containing only the essentials so that you can stash them in the shelter without taking up too much space.

Backup Power and Lighting

It's highly possible that power lines will be disrupted in the event of a nuclear disaster, so you're going to need flashlights, powerbanks, and plenty of long-life batteries (lithium and alkaline batteries last the longest). Remember to stock a variety of sizes and keep them in a dry, cool place. For other emergencies, I would probably recommend using rechargeable batteries that you can pair with a solar charger, but since you're going to need to stay inside and well away from windows unless you have a hand-operated charger or a good number of powerful chargers, this probably isn't the most practical solution. That said, I would recommend investing in some high-capacity power banks so you can charge your devices. You'll need to be able to listen for updates on the situation and stay in touch with family and friends as long as the lines remain open.

As for flashlights, if you've read *Prepare Your Home for a Sudden Grid-Down Situation,* you'll know that I'm a big fan of the Olight Warrior Mini 2 EDC Tactical Light, which lasts for about 164 hours before needing to be charged. There are plenty of options on the market—look for flashlights with the longest battery life so you don't need to tap into your power reserves so often. To light a broader area, it'd be a good idea to have an LED or battery-powered lantern. I have an Energizer 360 Pro, which takes standard batteries and can be charged externally. It'll run for 150 hours on its highest setting, which, as far as I'm aware, is hard to beat.

Clothes

If your shelter is underground, it's going to be cold, and even if you're using a fallout room in your house, you're going to need to turn the heating off if it pulls in air from the outside. There's also a good chance that the power will be out. All of this is to say you're going to need a good stash of warm clothes. Think in layers so that you can cool off and warm up as you need to.

Medical Supplies

A well-stocked first-aid kit is a must. You want to be able to treat any injuries or illnesses as they arise, and you're unlikely to be able to get medical help, at least until you're evacuated. I'd recommend that your whole family has some basic first aid training, but you can supplement this by making sure you have a first aid manual that will give you instructions on dealing with common medical emergencies and injuries.

Make sure you have a range of adhesive bandages of different sizes to treat blisters and cuts, as well as gauze and surgical tape for more severe wounds. You'll also want to make sure you have an antiseptic solution so that you can clean wounds and prevent them from becoming infected. Your first-aid kit should also include disposable gloves to avoid cross-contamination, scissors (for cutting tape and bandages), tweezers (for removing foreign objects like splinters), painkillers (obviously for reducing pain, but also to help manage fevers), a thermometer (which will help you keep track of your family's health), and an emergency blanket for anyone dealing with shock or extreme cold. You'll also want to have a good supply of all the personal medications used by your family, including medicines, devices, or equipment. Just as you do with your food and water supplies, you'll want to make sure you stay on top of the expiration dates and replace your stocks as you need to—and a word to the wise here: For a long time, I thought this only applied to medications and ointments, but your bandages have expiration dates too. They get more brittle as time goes on, and they're unable to absorb so much.

Important Documents

Make sure you have access to a copy of all of your important documents. You want to make sure you have passports and any other forms of photo ID, birth certificates, and all insurance forms. If there's any damage done to your house, these may not survive, and life after the disaster is going to be much easier if you have them.

Hygiene Products and Systems

Remember that your fallout room or shelter is the safest place you can be in the days following a nuclear incident, and this means that trips to the bathroom should be avoided. It would be wise to keep polythene buckets with well-fitting lids to use as an emergency toilet, as well as polythene bags so that you can empty them and a lidded trashcan to hold the waste. You'll also need plenty of toilet paper and some strong disinfectant, as well as hand sanitizer, to wash your hands. You can keep all of this just outside your shelter, along with a separate trashcan for any other domestic waste so that you keep the space hygienic.

Communication Supplies

We have no way of knowing what will and won't work during a nuclear disaster, and to a certain extent, it depends on the nature of the incident. However, communication is important, and we should do what we can to enable it, which means you should have a few key pieces of equipment in your survival kit. Firstly, you'll need a battery-operated radio so that you can listen for alerts (you could also opt for a hand-crank radio). This is how you'll know what's going on above ground and what the evacuation plans are going to be. Some radios have USB charging ports and flashlights, too, so if you choose wisely, you'll be able to cover a few bases with this. I'd also like to draw your attention to NOAA Weather Radio All Hazards (NWR), which is a network of stations that will broadcast not only weather information but all hazard information around the clock. Public safety alerts and post-event information will be broadcast here, and you'll be able to pick it up in the VHF public service band at the following frequencies (MHz): 162.400, 162.425, 162.450, 162.475, 162.500, 162.525, and 162.550 (National Weather Service n.d.).

I've mentioned walkie-talkies in previous books, and you might think this wouldn't be relevant here since you're going to need to stay in the shelter. However, this is something I still keep in my fallout room because you never know what might happen. What if you were separated during evacuation? It's important that there's a way for your group to communicate should you get separated. You'll want to choose walkie-talkies that have a long-range in case this happens. I'd also recommend having a whistle in case there comes a point when you need to signal for help.

Personal Protective Equipment (PPE)

PPE isn't something I've covered in other books because it's less relevant to other types of disaster, but when it comes to a nuclear emergency, it's definitely something you're going to want to have on hand.

Heavy clothing will help to protect you from alpha and beta radiation, but the same is not true for gamma radiation. The high-energy photons in gamma radiation will easily penetrate your clothing or even a serious protective suit like a HAZMAT suit (Weiner 2018). For this reason, I personally don't think it's worth investing in something like this. A better bet would be to wear thick clothing and stay as deep inside your shelter as possible until the worst is over. That said, you can buy shields that are designed to protect your most vulnerable tissue from gamma radiation. The 360 Gamma Shield is an example of this, but it's almost $3,000, and this certainly isn't something I can afford to buy for every member of my family. It's worth drawing attention to the fact that it exists, but the reality is that this is an unrealistic option for most people.

What will help, however, are respirators or gas masks and disposable gloves to minimize your exposure to radioactive material. You'll be able to find these, as well as respirators for children, online. They're not cheap, but you can get them for a few hundred dollars, which is certainly more realistic than several thousand. If you get something like this, you'll need to make sure that you equip it with filters designed to deal with nuclear particles.

Radiation Detector

A radiation detector is also specific to a nuclear emergency. If you have one of these, you'll be able to assess the surrounding area so that you can make informed decisions when you're weighing up whether it's safe to leave your shelter. A Geiger-Mueller counter is a good example of this. It's made up of a tube filled with gas-containing electrodes. When ionizing radiation moves through the tube, an electric current will pass between the electrodes in short pulses. You can tell how intense the radiation is by how many of these pulses there are within a second (United States Nuclear Regulatory Commission 2021). These are usually rechargeable and can be found online. We'll also look at some other options in Chapter 6.

Potassium Iodide

There's some debate about how helpful potassium iodide tablets will be in the event of a nuclear emergency. Potassium iodide (KI) is a non-radioactive type of iodine that can be taken to prevent radioactive iodine from being absorbed by the thyroid, thereby reducing the risk of thyroid cancer further down the line (CDC 2025). The CDC states that it's most effective taken just before or immediately after radioactive iodine enters the body, and they recommend it only for people under the age of 40 and those who are either pregnant or breastfeeding.

While it may offer protection against thyroid cancer for the restricted group who can take it, it should be noted that it only protects against radioactive iodine (and not other radioactive materials), and it only protects your thyroid. Radioactive iodine is more likely to be a concern if the disaster is related to a power plant; if there was a nuclear detonation, the radiation from the fallout would be our biggest concern, and there would be hundreds of different radioactive materials involved in this. Radioactive iodine would account for only 0.2% of what we might be exposed to (Business Insider 2022). Essentially, if you were exposed to radiation in this situation, you would have far bigger and more immediate concerns than the potential risk to your thyroid. I'll leave it up to you whether you want to include it in your supplies.

Other Items

There are several other things you'll want to make sure you have in your shelter, perhaps the top of the list being bedding. I doubt any of us will be terribly comfortable in this situation, but we can do what we can to make it as comfortable as possible. Make sure there's adequate bedding for everyone who will be using the shelter. If you're short on space, you might consider storing it in vacuum packs, opening them only when you need them, and packing the contents away during the day.

You'll also want a camping stove and essential kitchen supplies like saucepans, can openers, and utensils so that you can cook meals and boil water. I think a fire extinguisher would be a good plan, too. You're in a small space, and there could easily be an accident with that camping stove.

If you have an infant, you'll need a stockpile of diapers and baby formula, pets will need an adequate supply of food, and women of reproductive age will need a supply of feminine hygiene products. If you have children with you, some provisions to keep them occupied and help them pass the time would be advisable. We have a small selection of books, puzzles, and games ready for our kids, as well as paper and pencils for drawing. It would also be a good idea to include anything that will give them emotional support during a traumatic time. Perhaps they have a comfort blanket or a favorite stuffed animal that would help to soothe them. This is true of adults too, of course—my wife still has her childhood teddy bear, who she never travels without—there's no way he wouldn't be with her in the shelter, and I know he would bring her as much comfort as the kids' toys would bring them.

Last but not least, you'll need a bug-out bag for everyone in your family once evacuation is recommended. I'd refer you to *The Bug Out Book* for comprehensive details about what you'll want in one of these.

TRAINING YOURSELF FOR SURVIVAL

Building a stock of supplies is only half the story. You also want to make sure that you're mentally and physically prepared to survive a nuclear emergency, and that means stocking up on knowledge and skills. In this section, we'll take a brief look at some of the things you'll want to know how to do in the aftermath of a nuclear disaster, and we'll build on them throughout the book.

Purifying Water

I want to be clear here that open water in the vicinity of the disaster is going to be highly contaminated. It will still be safe to use it for washing because radiation in water is usually low, but it would be unwise to drink it unless you had no other option for survival (Burch 2023). While you're in your home, if you run out of your safe water supply, the first places to turn to are the toilet cistern (not the bowl) and the hot water tank, which have been stored inside your house and should be safe.

Once you've been evacuated, you may find yourself in need of a fresh supply of water, and if you're far enough away from the disaster site and need to rely on streams and lakes, you'll need to know something about how to purify water. You can only survive for three days without water (Macwelch 2019), and you want to make sure that the water you find is as safe as possible. In this section, we're going to look only at purifying water that you think is far enough away that you can trust it not to be contaminated by radiation; we'll look at what you may be able to do to remove radiation later in the book.

If you need to find safe water outdoors, your options are streams, lakes, ponds, creeks, and rainwater, but you'll need to rid whatever you collect of bacteria and parasites before you drink it. Your best option is to boil it for 10 minutes over a fire or camping stove in a fireproof container. If you don't have one, you can heat rocks in the fire for 30 minutes and add them to your water (Macwelch 2019). You could also invest in water purification tablets or a life straw for your bug-out bag. This filters the water as you drink and can even be connected to the drain valve on your water heater. It won't filter out everything, but it will make a difference. Remember, though, that none of this will remove the radiation—it's simply how you can remove other contaminants if you're far enough away from the site of the explosion.

Sourcing Food

Research from the University of Exeter has shown that crops grown close to Chornobyl were still contaminated over 30 years after the accident. Clearly, we're going to need to be careful about what we eat in the event of a nuclear disaster (Science Direct 2020). Food crops, the soil they grow in, and the crops with which we feed livestock are likely to be exposed to radioactive materials, and if you consume food like this, you'll raise the amount of radioactivity in your body, which will put your health at risk.

The good news is that not all our food will become contaminated. Anything that's already packaged and sealed in tins, jars, or plastic is likely to remain unharmed. This means your supplies should be safe to use, but you're also going to need to know what you can do once you've run out or if you need to evacuate and food is scarce.

Firstly, to protect any food you grow yourself, cover anything kept outside with plastic sheeting. Ventilation openings on greenhouses should be closed to protect your crops, and if you have animals, they can be sheltered in secure outhouses. If you have ripe crops, bring them inside and do what you can to preserve them in advance of a disaster. Once the fallout has happened, your food won't be safe to harvest (World Health

Organization 2023). Obviously, a nuclear incident could happen without warning, in which case, sheltering yourself and your family should be your only priority, and you will not have time to take these precautions; however, in the event that you're aware that the risk is high and you have time to prepare, it's worth doing what you can to protect your food sources.

Once you need to source food that you haven't stored safely yourself, it will be best to avoid any meat, vegetables, or dairy products that have been produced locally. This means you also don't want to forage for wild food (including aquatic plants and animals) anywhere near the disaster zone (World Health Organization 2023). All is not lost, though. There are a few things you can do to ensure your access to uncontaminated food.

Growing Food

As long as you're not very close to the blast, you may have the time to cover up your crops and soil. If you have plastic sheeting on hand, you'll be able to protect your vegetable plot, livestock, and any containers or outdoor equipment. Once you've been given the all-clear to come out of your initial shelter, if you're not evacuated, you'll need to clean all your gardening tools and improve your soil. Any plastic sheeting you've used to protect these things will need to be sealed in plastic bags and disposed of somewhere safe where they can't leak and cause further contamination. Make sure you wear gloves throughout this entire process and wash thoroughly every time you've been working outside.

Research after the incident at Fukushima told us a lot about what we can do to remove contamination from the soil. The advice is to remove the top 5-6 inches so that the soil will be safe for food production in the future and replace this with crushed gravel. This method was used in Fukushima, and it allowed for safe food to be grown later (Survival Garden Seeds 2022). You can also rebuild the top layer of soil by planting a cover crop straight away to nourish it. Remember to incorporate organic matter, as well as shredded cardboard or newspaper, straw, or peat moss.

This will all help your food production in the future, but you're going to need to eat in the meantime. Whether you're at home or you've had to evacuate, you may need to grow food indoors. This will also help you in the case of a nuclear winter, where it would be very difficult to grow food outside, even if the soil was safe. One thing you can do as soon as you have to take shelter is start growing microgreens, which will be ready to harvest after a couple of weeks. For this, you'll need your seeds, growing trays (food storage containers with holes made in the bottoms for drainage will work in a pinch), covers, a growing medium (this could be potting compost or foam), and a water mister to keep your plants moist without overwhelming them. You can make this work if you have no power, but you're even more likely to be successful if you also have grow lights, heat mats, fans for ventilation, and a grow rack (so you can fit more in your space). If you've planned your emergency power sources carefully, you should be able to keep these things running.

Microgreens are the quickest thing you can grow indoors, but you can also grow more long-term plants. Root vegetables, green leafy vegetables, cruciferous vegetables, peppers, tomatoes, and herbs can all be grown successfully indoors. Mushrooms and potatoes will even work if you don't have much light. I've personally never grown much food indoors before, but I'm working on these skills now in case they become necessary—and I've already had quite a lot of success with microgreens.

Hunting and Trapping

Animals near the disaster site are likely to have been exposed to radiation, so you're not going to be hunting anywhere near your first place of shelter. However, in the post-nuclear world, you may find that hunting and trapping your own meat and fish becomes necessary, so these are skills that it would be wise to learn now.

Since you'll be practicing a lot, focus your sights on animals who live in environments where you won't mind spending a lot of time—you may as well enjoy the process while you're learning! Most states require you to take a hunter education course (as well as a hunter safety course) before they allow you to buy a license, and while a license won't be your most pressing concern when you're in a survival situation, you will need one while you're training (US Fish and Wildlife Service n.d.). The advantage of this is that you'll learn the fundamentals of hunting along the way, no matter how much of a beginner you are. You'll need to research the licensing process in your state, too. In some states, there are lotteries for them; they open well before the hunting season, and the fees can vary wildly between states (Fohrman 2020).

Beyond this, absorb all the hunting information you can. Watch videos online about what to do with an animal once you've successfully killed it; take online courses; consume as much media about hunting as possible. You might also want to find a mentor who can share their wisdom and get you up to speed quickly.

Food Preservation

You're going to want to build up your skills in food preservation, both for the sake of building your stockpile and so that you have these skills in a post-nuclear world. The goal is simply to slow down food deterioration and prevent bacterial growth while preserving the nutritional content and flavor of foods. You'll find much more detail about this in *The Prepper's Pantry*, but I'll give you an overview of your options here:

- **Freezing:** This process stops the growth of bacteria so you can keep it for longer. Food should be frozen in airtight bags or containers at between -0.4°F and -7.6°F (Coleman 2024). The drawback of freezing is that if the power goes out, you're going to lose your stocks very quickly, and if you have to evacuate, you won't be able to take it with you. In order to prepare properly for a nuclear emergency, you're going to need to rely on other methods of food preservation.
- **Salting:** This will draw water from food to prevent bacteria from growing and is usually known as "curing."

In dry curing, you salt the food directly, while in wet curing, you create a brine by mixing salt into water and then bathing the food in it.

- **Sugaring:** This reduces the water content of a food, thereby limiting the amount of bacteria that can grow. You can use sugar granules, honey, molasses, or sugar syrup to do this, and it works best for turning fruits and vegetables into jams and relishes. You can also add sugar to brine to preserve meat and fish.
- **Canning:** This process removes the oxygen from the food and prevents bacteria growth by packing it in an airtight environment with sugar, salt, or acid. You'll need to use canning jars for this so that you're sure they're airtight, and health and hygiene must be at the forefront of your mind. The C. botulinum bacteria are like oxygen-free environments, and you'll need to make sure your jars are properly sterilized and that any bacteria has been killed before you add your food (Coleman 2024).
- **Freeze-drying:** This is a way to dehydrate food to remove its water content. Food is frozen under pressure and dried out in two stages, first to remove the frozen water and then to remove the bound water that still remains after freezing.
- **Vacuum Packing:** Again, this removes the oxygen to prevent bacteria growth. Unlike canning, however, you don't need to add any other ingredients, so anything you preserve in this way will taste and smell just the same as it would have done if you'd eaten it fresh. This is another one where you have to be mindful of C.

botulinum, though. Make sure you follow all instructions carefully.

Natural Medicine

When commercial medication is scarce, herbal remedies can help you deal with common illnesses and ailments, but you'll need to feel confident in your knowledge first. I'd advise reading dedicated books on the topic and maybe even taking a short course to build your knowledge and confidence, but here are a few of the most helpful herbs you may be able to access (although remember that you should never gather these from anywhere near to the site of the accident as they will have been exposed to radiation):

- **Chamomile:** This can reduce anxiety and aid relaxation, but it can also be used to treat wounds and reduce swelling and inflammation. It can be drunk as a tea or applied to an injured area or rash as a compress.
- **Echinacea:** The leaves, stalks, and roots of this plant can be used to treat infections and common illnesses like colds and the flu, and it can also help wounds heal. It's only recommended for short-term use, though, because it can affect your immune system (University of Rochester Medical Center, n.d.).
- **Garlic:** There's more to garlic than its flavor, and my wife, as a nutritionist, has drummed its benefits into me. It can protect your heart, fight germs, and reduce inflammation. Try to keep plenty of it in your supplies

so that you can add more of it to your food if someone in your family gets sick.
- **Ginger:** This is great for reducing nausea, and it has high anti-inflammatory benefits. It's also very good for your immune system, so if you're able to make ginger tea regularly, you'll reduce your chances of getting sick and nip illnesses in the bud more quickly (Kubala 2023).
- **Goldenseal:** This can help with diarrhea and skin irritations, and it can also be used as an antiseptic. It must be used cautiously, though, because it can irritate the skin or the stomach, and in high doses, it can be poisonous (University of Rochester Medical Center n.d.).

You need to know what you're doing before you use any herb as a remedy. Some are unsafe to use in tandem with other medications, and the dosage is important. Now is the time to learn; that way, you're prepared for the future.

First Aid for Radiation Sickness and Injuries

Fundamental first aid skills are something everyone should have, and it's even appropriate for children of a certain age to learn them. Everyone in my family has basic first aid training, and my wife and I have always viewed this as an important survival skill that we were determined for our children to have. To prepare for a nuclear disaster, however, you're going to need some more specific skills.

Acute exposure to ionizing radiation can lead to radiation sickness, which we'll look at in more detail later in the book. In an ideal world, it will be treated by a medical professional, but you may not have access to this support. If you're in a situation where you're required to give first aid to someone who has been exposed to radiation, protect yourself first and try to decontaminate the patient as much as possible. You'll then need to check their pulse and breathing so that you can begin CPR if needed. Remove their clothing and seal it inside a container to prevent ongoing contamination, and then wash them vigorously with soap and water. Once the patient is dry, wrap them in a clean blanket to keep them warm. Make sure to do all of these tasks well away from the place in which the patient was exposed to radiation, change your own clothing, and wash thoroughly (Mount Sinai n.d.).

You may also have to deal with radiation injuries like burns, ulcers, or blisters (Turai and Veress, 2001). Again, remove the patient from the place where they were exposed as quickly as you can, and take the same precautionary measures as you would take for treating radiation sickness. These injuries can then be cleaned and bandaged, but avoid putting any creams or ointments onto burns (Mount Sinai n.d.).

Starting a Fire Without Matches

You don't know for sure what your situation will be after evacuation, and it's possible that you'll be stuck outside with a high need for warmth and the ability to cook. For this, you'll need to be able to start a fire, and it's worth knowing how to do this without matches so that you'll never be caught out. Again, this is something I'd recommend delving into further, but here's an overview of your options (Goldbach 2024):

- Gather dry leaves, sticks, and grass for tinder, and create friction to set it alight by rubbing two pieces of dry wood together until they spark. You could also create this spark by rubbing both prongs on a 9-volt battery against some steel wool or focusing sunlight through glass. Once you've created a spark, blow gently on the source to help the flame grow before transferring it to the tinder. You'll then need to blow this gently so that it catches light. From here, you can add larger pieces of wood (make sure they're dry) to build a fire.

- Lay char cloth or charcoal on top of a piece of flint and strike a blade along it quickly until you see a spark. You can usually find flint in river beds, and you'll know it by its glassy gray or black surface. Again, you'll need to build a nest of tinder first, and once you see the sparks, you can catch them with your char cloth. This will then glow, resembling an ember, and can be transferred to the tinder. Blow on this gently until you see a flame growing.

- Make a spindle to create friction against wood. Source a piece of wood and cut a V-shaped notch in the middle. Find some small pieces of bark to put beneath this and a stick to use as a spindle. You'll want this to be about 5 inches wide. Place it into the notch and rub it between your hands, pressing down into the wood until you see embers. These can then be transferred to your tinder and blown on gently until a flame starts to grow.

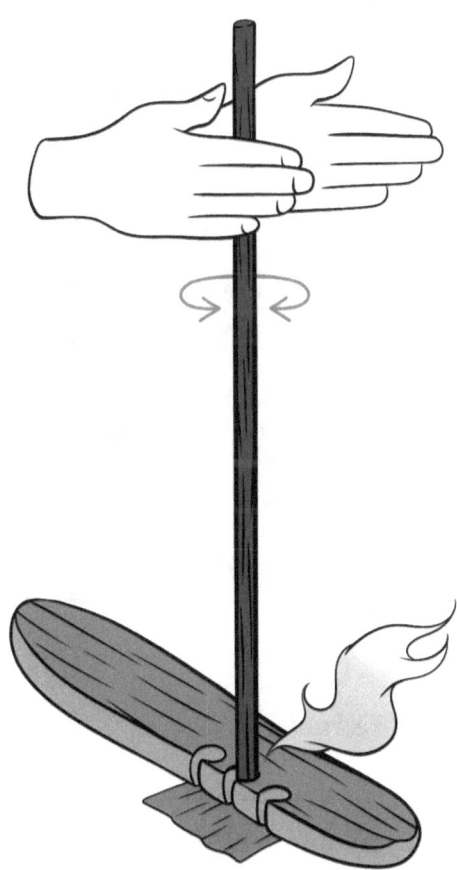

- Use a bendy stick and string to make a bow. You can use shoelaces or string for this, but if you have neither, the roots of a plant will work. Attach this to both ends of your stick, and source a piece of wood that you can use for the base. Again, cut a V-shaped notch into this and place a tinder over it. Put the stick in the center of the notch, holding it steady with a rock, and move the bow as you would a saw until you see a flame.

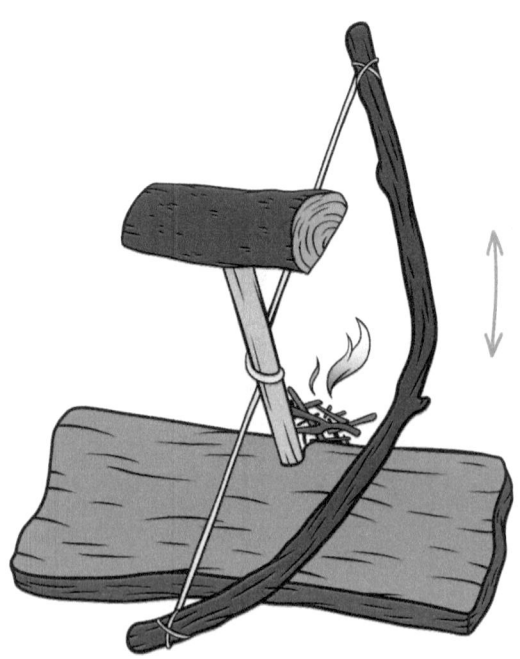

Navigating Without Technology

If you find yourself traveling across an area you don't know (or an area that looks very different since the blast), you may need navigational skills. You may not be able to rely on your phone

CHAPTER 4 | 75

at this time, so you need some more traditional methods up your sleeve. I haven't included any method in this list that may not be reliable if the landscape is destroyed by the blast. Here are some skills that will be helpful (Mertins n.d.):

- **Use the sun.** Assuming you're in the northern hemisphere, the sun will be at its highest point when it's in the south, so all you need to do is pay attention to its path and find the point where it's at its highest. This will tell you which direction south is in, and from here, you'll be able to identify the other compass points.

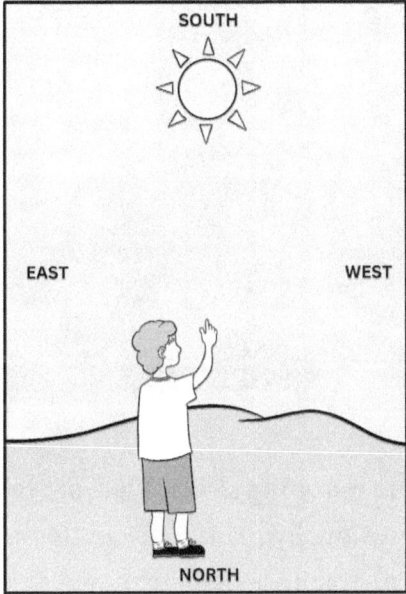

- **Use the stars.** Start by locating the big dipper (familiarize yourself with this now if you don't know how to recognize it). Then, look for the front of its scoop and visualize a line running between the two stars at the front and continuing beyond it. This will show you where the north star is: It's the bright star that lines up with the front of the constellation if you keep following the line. Face this star, and you'll know you're facing north.

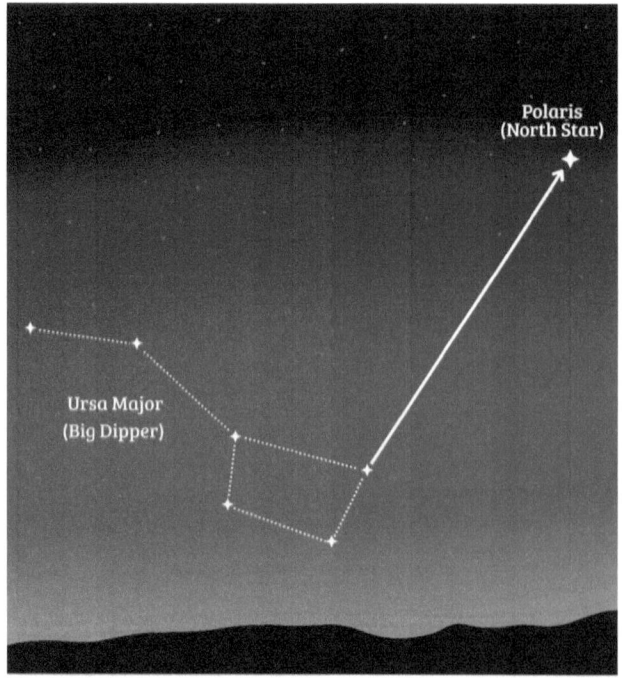

- **Sharpen your mapping skills.** I haven't included reading professionally made maps in this section because there's a chance that you could be navigating a devastated landscape. However, if you practice your skills in mapping now, you'll be able to create your own as you get to know a new area, and this could be extremely helpful. Explore the area and identify landmarks that will help you find your way. This could be anything from trees to abandoned buildings or vehicles. Draw all of these and your route through them to create a map. While you're brushing up on this skill, you'll want to make as many of these maps as you can. You'll probably find that your memory isn't always reliable, and not everything you remember makes it back to your map accurately.

- **Build your general awareness.** The more you practice paying attention to your surroundings now, the more likely it is that you'll be able to navigate a new area. Practice focusing your awareness whenever you're out and about, paying attention to every feature. This means being aware of whether you're going downhill or uphill, remembering the direction from which you came, and noticing any landmarks you pass. This skill will serve you if you're navigating unfamiliar territory.

Basic Self-Defense Moves

The reason I bring up self-defense is simply because we could find ourselves in a desperate situation, and you can't predict someone's behavior when all they're focused on is their own survival. As you'll know if you've read my other books, I'm not a big fan of firearms, and I have no desire to attack anyone else, no matter what I'm in need of. I do, however, realize that I may need to protect myself if someone were to attack me, and for this, the best solution is martial arts training. I'd highly recommend signing up for a class, but as a starting point, here are five moves that it would be helpful to learn (Swenson 2022):

- **Use your knees and elbows to knock someone off you.** You might think that your fists would be helpful, but this could very easily result in injury, so you want to use your knees and elbows.
- **Kick your attacker.** Your legs are longer than your arms, which will give you more range, and they're stronger, too. You can use kicks to the front, to the side, or around your body, and all of these can be picked up by learning about a martial art.
- **Use a rear naked chokehold.** This comes from Brazilian Jiu-Jitsu and allows you to gain control over your attacker. The principle is that you slide your arm around their neck and hold on to the bicep on your other arm, which will secure their head and prevent them from attacking you further (Jiu-Jitsu Brotherhood n.d.).
- **Strike them with your palm or scratch them.** This gives you a less dangerous option than using your fist and risking injury, and it might be enough to deter them.
- **Run.** There's no shame in removing yourself from the situation, and sometimes, the best option is simply to run away. Keep your fitness up now, and this will be easier and more effective if you ever need to rely on it.

Alternative Communication Methods

There's a high chance that you won't be able to rely on the communication methods you're used to, so you'll need to have backup options. Here are a few for you to look into:

- **Ham Radio:** You do need a license for this, but it's such an effective means of communicating when you're off the grid that I'd definitely recommend it. Getting mine brought me huge peace of mind. A ham radio transmits and receives signals through antennas, and when conditions are optimal, it can reach someone hundreds of miles away. Because it can pick up a variety of radio frequencies, you'll also be able to tune into emergency communications and radio broadcasts.
- **CB Radio (Citizens Band Radio):** This is useful for communicating over a shorter distance. Truckers tend to use it, and there's no license required. It operates on 40 channels and transmits and receives signals through handheld devices, which would make it helpful for communicating with the rest of your party if you're split up.
- **Satellite Phones:** These connect to satellites and can communicate with other phones anywhere in the world. They're quite expensive, but you can keep your costs down by choosing a device that will only transmit your location and send short messages. I have a Garmin Inreach Explorer, and I'm confident that it would be enough to help me in an emergency.
- **Walkie-talkies:** These are useful for short-range communication, and they're very easy to use. Radio signals are received and transmitted between devices, and their range will usually cover a few miles, depending on the obstacles in the way. Again, these would be helpful for communicating with other members of your group.

- **Low-Tech Options:** I think it's always worth knowing the most basic methods of anything because tech can easily break down. Learn about how to use flares, mirrors, whistles, Morse code signals, and smoke signals to show that you're in distress if your other methods of communication prove unreliable.

Bartering

We have no idea what a post-nuclear world may look like, but the chances are, if it comes to this, bartering is going to be a very helpful skill. It's what we used before we exchanged currency, and it allows us to exchange services and goods for things that we need more. Firstly, it's important to be aware that it comes with risk, and in an ideal world, you'll barter only with people you trust. You may not have this option, though, so be ready to assess the situation and decide whether offering a trade is worth the risk. You'll also want to be sure that you're not offering to trade something you may need later, so it's important to be able to distinguish between needs and wants.

The things that will be of the most value are those that will help people meet their basic survival needs; if they already have these, they'll be interested in things that make them more comfortable. Your best bet is to be able to offer a skill; this will allow you to trade your time rather than something that could become essential for you later. Skills like DIY skills, carpentry, sewing, cooking, hunting, and nursing are all examples of valuable skills, but really, anything that could solve a problem for someone else could be useful. I'd recommend building up your skills in something that interests you, giving you a chance to explore a personal project, and making yourself indispensable in a crisis.

As far as goods go, anything you have could be something that someone needs. I'd recommend protecting any supplies that you have no way of producing yourself and offering only things you can do without or will be able to get again easily. Food, water, clothing, cooking supplies, sanitation and medical supplies, garden tools, communication and power devices, survival equipment, and alcohol may all be valuable items to someone else.

Waste and Hygiene Management

Wherever you find yourself, you need to be able to protect your family's health and safety, and for this, you'll need to be prepared to take care of waste, both human and otherwise.

If you're somewhere with a toilet but the water supply is cut off, you'll be able to manage human waste very easily, as long as you have enough water to fill the tank between flushes. Instigate a policy in which you only flush when necessary so that you can preserve your supply. If you're unable to access a toilet, aim to keep solid waste separate from urine to make it easier to dispose of. A lidded bucket will make a sufficient emergency toilet that you can then empty into a pit outside. For fecal matter, it's a good idea to add sawdust, torn-up newspaper, or dry grass after each use to manage the odor. Make sure you bury it well when you empty it, and do so a good distance away from where you're eating and sleeping. Remember, though, that while you're unable to leave the shelter, you won't be able to do this. In this case, make sure your waste is sealed inside a container and left just outside the entrance to your shelter so that you can deal with it when it's safe to do so.

As for your other trash, you may find that more of it is useful than you realize. Paper may be needed for emergency toilet paper (crumple it until it softens if you intend to do this, though), jars can be used for other purposes, and tins can be used as cooking pots. Be sure to thoroughly clean anything you intend to use again. Anything you definitely want to throw away can then be buried.

If you need to be on the move, the same principles apply. Urine is relatively easy to manage, as any camper knows. To dispose of feces, you'll need to dig a hole at least 6 inches down and bury the waste. For trash, you'll either have to carry it with you or bury it. If you find yourself bugging out in one spot, your best bet for managing human waste is to dig a latrine, which is essentially just a deep, narrow hole. Make sure it's downhill (and downwind) from your shelter and a minimum of 50 yards away from your water supply (MacWelch 2019). Keep it covered when you're not using it, and cover the waste with earth after each use.

Building Your Mental Resilience

As we saw in earlier chapters, you're likely to be faced with significant psychological challenges in the event of a nuclear disaster. This means that building your mental resilience is one of the best ways you can prepare. Research shows that people with a high degree of mental resilience possess certain traits that are helpful during difficult times (Sutton 2024):

- An ability to persevere in spite of challenges
- A high level of self-belief, even when there's a lot of pressure
- The ability to concentrate when there are many distractions or a lot of pressure
- An ability to bounce back from failures and obstacles
- High emotional awareness and an ability to stay calm
- Dedication to achieving a goal
- An ability to adapt quickly to new circumstances
- The ability to stay positive and view a challenge as an opportunity
- Self-motivation
- The ability to use stress to their advantage

If you feel that you struggle with any of these things, these are the skills you need to start working on now in order to improve your mental resilience and protect your psychological health in an emergency. I'll admit that I've had to work on some of this myself, and one of the things that's worked best for me is setting myself goals and evaluating how I've responded to the process of achieving them. If your struggle is with positive thinking, practicing positive affirmations might help you, as well as reframing things that you view as negative as positives.

Of course, it isn't only your own mental resilience you need to be concerned with. If you have children, you'll need to prepare them, too. You want them to be able to face challenges with confidence and cope well in stressful situations. Every child is different, and it may be that what works with one won't work with another, but here are some tips you could try to help your kids with this (Sutton 2024):

- Teach them what negative thoughts are so that they recognize them and encourage them to replace them with positive ones.
- Help them to be aware of their emotions, and give them techniques that will help them regulate them.
- Model what resilience looks like. If they see you overcoming challenges, learning from your mistakes, and taking a positive outlook, they'll start to do it themselves.
- Allow them to be independent. Give them opportunities to solve problems and make decisions for themselves.
- Teach them how to break problems down to make them more manageable and do the same with overwhelming tasks.
- Help them to develop a growth mindset, and show them that every mistake is an opportunity to learn more and do better next time.
- Be careful not to only praise them for their successes; praise them for the effort they put in, too. This will encourage them to continue to put this effort into things they find challenging, even if they're not confident in their abilities.
- Encourage them to face their fears. Obviously, you don't want to scare them, but with your support, they can learn to tolerate some level of discomfort and experience the reward of having done this.

Make a Family Emergency Plan

It's possible that any plans you have will go out the window if the situation is extreme, but it's wise to have a plan in place nonetheless. You may be told where you'll be evacuated, but you should have a plan for a safe place you can get to in case you're left to fend for yourself. Your emergency plan should include a meeting point (in case you all have to shelter in different places in the immediate aftermath of the incident) and an out-of-state contact whom you can keep posted on your safety. It should also include the means by which you expect to receive emergency alerts, what your shelter plan is, what route you'll take if you have to evacuate, and how you'll communicate as a family if you get separated. Make sure you take into account the specific needs of everyone in your family when you come up with your plan.

Your children should know about this plan. In Chapter 5, we'll look more closely at how to talk to them about nuclear emergencies, but they should know a little something about the threat. They'll probably have lots of questions. Try to reassure them and give them information that will help them if you do need to use the emergency plan. Children should always know how to make an emergency call, which may not help in a nuclear disaster, but it's a good thing to cover with them anyway. My kids now have a good grasp of our emergency plan, but when they were younger, we revisited it every six months or so to make sure they knew our meeting point and what safety rules they should follow.

TAKE ACTION!

Use the following template to create your family emergency plan:

Household Information

    Address

Family Members

    Name
    Mobile Number
    Email
    Medical Information

(Repeat this for each person.)

Emergency Plans

(Enter information about workplaces, caregivers, childcare, and schools here.)

    Name
    Address
    Contact number
    Website
    Emergency pick-up plan

Emergency Contacts

    Name
    Address
    Phone Number
    Email

Emergency Meeting Places

    Location
    Additional Instructions

Medical Information

    Doctor Name
    Doctor Number
    Vet Name
    Vet Number
    Medication and allergy information
    Medical Insurance Name
    Medical Insurance Policy Number

A family emergency plan is going to need everyone to know about it and understand exactly what to do. This isn't always an easy conversation to have, so in the next chapter, we'll look at how to go about it, but not before we take a quick diversion to consider how we can share our belief in being prepared with the wider world.

BUILDING A POST-NUCLEAR SURVIVAL COMMUNITY

"Opportunity does not waste time with those who are unprepared."

— IDOWU KOYENIKAN.

There will always be people who don't see your point of view and think your determination to prepare for potential disasters is too extreme. We'll take a look at how to approach conversations with these people in the next chapter, but for now, let's think about the great many who do understand your point of view.

It comes as no surprise that there's an increasing interest in information about how to prepare for a nuclear disaster. Nuclear issues are never far from the news, and there's an increasing risk of disasters that could be prevented. This makes many of us want to prepare, and there isn't a lot of information out there that will help us to do that.

To an extent, this is because it's difficult to know exactly what the world will look like in some scenarios, which means that it's impossible to cover the topic as fully as I'd like. But I hope that what I'm doing with my own family and sharing with you here is enough to reassure you that there are some steps you can take now to prepare for a potential disaster. What I'd like to ask you to do now is join me in spreading this information further and helping me to reach more of the people who share our point of view. The good news is that this is very easy. All you have to do is leave a short review.

By leaving a review of this book on Amazon, you'll make it easy for other readers who want to prepare for a nuclear emergency to find it.

The more of us who have the resources and skills to survive in this situation, the better off the world will be if the unthinkable happens. In essence, we're building a post-nuclear survival community now—and that's only going to help us later.

I greatly appreciate your support—thank you. Now, let's return to helping communicate this message to the people directly involved in your life—in particular, your children.

Scan the QR code below to leave your review.

5

THE CONVERSATIONS NO ONE WANTS TO HAVE—HOW TO PREPARE YOUR FAMILY

Survival and preparedness have been a part of my life since I was younger than my own kids are now, and this meant that it came naturally to me to talk to my family about potentially scary situations. I was cautious in my approach, though: I built their understanding gradually, simply by explaining to them why we do everything the way we do it at a level they could understand. I know this isn't easy for everyone, especially if you're only getting into survival preparedness now, but it's important. When you draw up your family emergency plan, your family needs to understand what it's for and why it might be necessary, and the best way of minimizing panic if the worst-case scenario happens, is to make sure everyone is properly prepared beforehand—including children.

TALKING ABOUT SURVIVAL

I wouldn't start by bringing up the specifics of nuclear dangers right away. The best place to start is with survival in general; that way, your family will understand the underlying principles before you get to the scary stuff.

The first thing to be aware of is to keep it positive. Focus more on the survival part than on the disaster part. It's true that it's helpful to be aware of the things that could happen and why certain skills are relevant at different times, but if you focus too much on the disasters, you run the risk of putting your family into a negative mindset. You can actually make it fun, and when you include activities that will help them sharpen their survival skills, they'll have a hands-on experience that will automatically make them more engaged and eager to soak up the information you want them to know.

With your children, you'll need to keep it simple and pitched at an appropriate level for their age. Talk about the sorts of disasters that might happen and what your family would need to do if they did, trying to relate this to experiences that they're familiar with. This doesn't need to be a big sit-down talk; you can work it into ordinary conversations, involving them in each part of the discussion. If your partner has the same mindset as you, this should be relatively easy.

This may not be the case, though. If your partner doesn't understand your desire to be prepared, you may first need to explain your reasoning to them, bringing up examples of disasters that have already happened and relating them to how your own family would cope if they happened to you. It might help to compare it to buying insurance: All you're trying to do is make sure you have insurance in place for any future disaster. Avoid starting with the worst-case scenarios, and try to get them to see that prepping isn't just about preparing for a disaster—it helps us to prepare you for any unexpected event like the loss of income or an illness that changes the way you have to live your life.

When it comes to your extended family or any friends you'd like to encourage, my wife and I have found that gifting works quite well. We've put together first aid kits and home canning kits as Christmas gifts in the past, and it's made it easy to start the conversation and get them thinking about the value of being prepared. We've even gotten a few friends obsessed with canning that way! You could also give them a book on emergency preparedness (I can think of a few you might know of!) Of course, there'll always be some people who just won't come around to your way of thinking, and although that can be disheartening, you'd be better off focusing your energy on your immediate family.

Talking About Your Family Emergency Plan

Talking about preparing for potential disasters is really just the beginning. The next thing to do is make sure that everyone knows about your family emergency plan. Now that you've laid the groundwork, you might want to talk to your kids about the warning signs of different disasters so that they'll be less scared if they happen and have some idea about how you'll need to respond. You'll also want to make sure they know what to do in an emergency. All children should know how to call 911, and older children should know how to contact you if they're home alone. I'd recommend having your numbers on the fridge or somewhere where they can easily see them. You can even do this with younger children, using pictures to show who the numbers relate to if they can't read. They may not be home alone at this age, but if Dad has an accident and Mom's at work, for example, you want them to know what to do. You can also talk to them about the sorts of people that can help in a disaster—people like police officers, Red Cross workers, firefighters, and doctors. You should have an out-of-state contact on your family emergency plan, too, so make sure they know who this is and how they should contact them if they can't reach your partner or you. We helped our kids memorize all the most important numbers, but if this isn't your child's strong suit, you could always make a number card that they carry with them. Make sure they know where you'll meet in the event of an emergency and what your plans are, and revisit this every few months to make sure they still remember. Again, try to stay positive and reassuring, and remind them that you'll be with them if you ever have to use this emergency plan. This should allay some of their fears.

EMERGENCY CHECKLIST

Emergency
911 Police, Fire, Ambulance

Parent or Guardian #1
Name: **Mom – Kate Riley**
Phone: **(555) 123-4567**

Parent or Guardian #2
Name: **Dad – Ted Riley**
Phone: **(555) 234-5678**

Out-of-State Contact
Name: **Aunty Jenny (Lives in Oregon)**
Phone: **(503) 555-7890**

Trusted Neighbor
Name: **Mr. Jenkins (Next door)**
Phone: **(555) 345-6789**

Backup Caregiver
Name: **Grandma Maria**
Phone: **(212) 555-9876**

Home Address
123 Sunshine Lane, Pleasantville, NY 10570

School Contact
Name: **Ms. Thompson (Principal)**
Phone: **(555) 456-7890**

Doctor
Name: **Dr. Phil Good – Family Pediatrician**
Phone: **(555) 567-8901**

Emergency Meeting Spot
Big tree at Miller Park (Across from school)

TRAINING YOUR FAMILY

The next part of getting every member of your family prepared is making sure that they have the skills and knowledge they need to help them in a crisis. The first thing I'd say about this is to make it fun, again focusing on the positives rather than on the frightening reasons why they might one day need to use these skills.

Obviously, exactly what you can teach your children depends on their ages and levels of maturity. You can't teach a two-year-old how to start a fire, but this is definitely something you could do with a ten-year-old. Consider their interests and abilities, and use this information to find segues into teaching them survival skills. Here are some of the most important lessons I think you can teach them:

- **Belief in Their Ability to Deal with a Problem:** As we all know, you have to believe you can do something before you're able to do it successfully, and with your kids, this starts with *your* belief in them. This is something you can weave into their everyday lives simply by allowing them to tackle challenges and find solutions to problems and encouraging them along the way. You can play games to do this, too. We've always enjoyed playing the *What If* game in my family, coming up with a scenario and brainstorming possible solutions. When you do this, your kids have to identify the problem, investigate different options for dealing with it, and see themselves overcoming the challenge. It not only builds their problem-solving skills; it also builds their confidence that they can deal with a challenging situation if it arises.

- **What to Do If Different Disasters Occur:** You already have a family emergency plan; make sure you use it to prepare your children. They should know exactly where to meet if you're not all together, and there should be backup plans in case something goes wrong. I'd recommend practicing going through the steps of your emergency plan regularly.
- **To Be in Good Physical Shape:** In an emergency situation, they may need to walk some distance, and you want them to be fit enough to be able to handle this. All this requires is making time for regular family walks and hiking trips—and, of course, any fun family sports activities you might want to add into the mix.
- **How to Use First Aid Equipment and Techniques:** Make sure they know exactly what's in your first aid kit, what it's designed for, and how to use it. You want them to know how to handle pains and rashes, how to dress a wound, and once they're old enough, how to deal with serious injuries and save a life. There are first aid courses designed specifically for children if you're concerned about how to teach them these skills.
- **How to Forage for Food, Source Safe Drinking Water, and Start a Fire:** Family camping trips are the best way to teach skills like these because they're a fun part of camping anyway, and it means you can teach them fundamental survival skills without them focusing on any kind of disaster scenario in which they might need

to use them. Camping is a great time to teach sanitation and hygiene lessons when the creature comforts aren't available, too.

- **Basic Self-Defense Skills:** Hopefully, they'll never need to use them, but you want to know that they could protect themselves if they needed to. I think the best thing to do here is to sign them up for martial arts classes. These teach discipline, too, and they can do a great job of building a child's confidence.
- **Emergency Life Skills:** With the basics in place, you can then go on to teach them how to adapt these skills in potential emergencies. For example, once they have some basic cooking skills, you can teach them ways to cook without electricity and how to cook the foods you have in your supplies in case of an emergency. You'll always need to rotate your supplies anyway, so when it's time to use something up and replace it, take the opportunity to cook it with your child. You can also teach them about how to grow, harvest, and store food, different methods of keeping warm, how to use emergency lighting, and how to use all the communication equipment you have in your bug-out bag.
- **How to Use Their Survival Kit:** Everyone in your family should have a bug-out bag (and I'll refer you to *The Bug Out Book* for more details on how to build one), but they should also know how to use it. Have them help you pack their bag, and make sure they know how to use everything in it. Again, camping trips give you a good opportunity to do this.

- **Fire Safety:** Open flames are a likely part of any survival situation, whether it's lighting a fire, using a candle, or operating emergency cooking equipment. Children need to know how to use fire safely and what to do in the case of an accident. When you're teaching them how to use cooking equipment that uses gas, be sure to teach them about carbon monoxide and gas safety, too.
- **How to Self-Soothe and Release Stress:** If a disaster of any kind strikes, it's going to be stressful. Teach your kids breathing and meditation techniques that they can turn to whenever they feel their stress rising—it will help them out in general life, too.
- **Basic Legal and Financial Knowledge:** It's easy to overlook this, but your children should know where to find all your important legal documents in case something were to happen to you. They should also know where your emergency funds are and how to use them wisely. Financial management and access to financial resources are life skills you'll want to give them anyway, so you can incorporate this as part of those lessons.

WHAT TO DO WHEN THEY DON'T TAKE IT SERIOUSLY

Children aren't the problem here so much. They'll have fun learning all the skills you're teaching them, especially if the focus isn't on disaster planning. However, you may have older family members or friends who don't share your beliefs and are difficult to get on board with when preparing for an emergency. They may see the value in being prepared but lack the sense of urgency to do anything about it immediately. I find the best strategy in this situation is to draw attention to scenarios that highlight that urgency without relating it to your own plans. If they can see an immediate need and come to that conclusion themselves, they're more likely to put disaster planning higher up on their priority list.

When you're talking to people who don't see the value of emergency preparedness, you're liable to hear a lot of counterarguments—prepping is costly or difficult, for example, or that disaster may never strike. Make sure you have an answer for these up your sleeve so that they don't have further fuel for their resistance. Beyond this, I'd simply suggest you do what you can to prepare around them. You may want them on your side, but if they're not, at least you can still make sure you're prepared and focus your energy on this.

TALKING ABOUT NUCLEAR DISASTERS

A nuclear disaster is a specific kind of emergency situation, so you'll want your kids to know about this, too. It's a scary subject, though, and you're going to need to bring it up without terrifying them. Once they're comfortable with the idea of the need to be prepared for an emergency, you can bring up this more difficult topic. Prepare for the conversation carefully—you don't want to spring it on them and terrify them. Talking about any difficult subject often gives rise to strong emotions, so be prepared to navigate these gently as they come up.

Children and adults are both likely to express fear, sadness, or anxiety when you're talking about the potential for a nuclear disaster, and it's important not to dismiss their emotions. Most people find it reassuring if you acknowledge their emotions in the moment; it makes them feel seen and heard, and it can go a long way toward making them feel calmer.

Think carefully about a good time and place to have this conversation, which may well depend on the personalities in your family. Some people find it easier to have big conversations when they're walking; others prefer to feel safe and comfortable at home. With children especially, try to make the conversation relevant to them. You might be able to find something in a TV show or a favorite movie that would give you an easy inroad—like the green sludge in *The Simpsons*, for example. Perhaps you can even relate it to something they've been learning about in school. They're bound to have questions and concerns, so give them the space to voice these, and make sure they know they can always talk to you if they have additional worries later.

You might worry about whether it's a good idea to bring up the subject of nuclear disasters at all, but you do want them to be mentally prepared. As far as the nuclear tensions we're already seeing in the world go, experts recommend telling children the truth (Italie 2022). They've probably already heard pieces of information about this, and if they've ever tried to look it up for themselves, they may have come across unhelpful misinformation. You can use news stories as a springboard for these discussions; the chances are the open conversation will work to ease fears you didn't realize they were already experiencing.

DEALING WITH ANXIETY

I don't mind admitting that thinking about and researching nuclear war, in particular, has given me some anxiety, and it's highly possible that these conversations may have a similar effect on other members of your family. You may find that you all feel uncertain or stressed out at times. I'd recommend focusing on what you can control, and that's your preparedness plan. Make sure your family lifestyle supports stress reduction by eating well, prioritizing sleep, and spending time together as a unit. Talk to your family about the value of self-care, and model what this looks like by taking the time you need to look after your own mental health.

It's natural to find it difficult to think about the potential of a nuclear disaster, especially one driven by war. Something as serious as this will lead to widespread suffering and long-lasting consequences that could change life as we know it completely. While you do want to be prepared for the possibility, what you don't want to do is fall into a cycle of constant worry. Remind yourself that this hasn't happened, and there's a good chance that it won't in your lifetime. I find breathing techniques help me to calm my thoughts and come back to a more relaxed state—you'll find many effective ones if you search online.

TAKE ACTION!

One of the best things you can do to get your kids into a prepping mindset is to play games with them. Here are a few I've tried with my own family over the years.

- **Road Trip!** Everyone has 15 minutes to pack their bug-out bag and get ready to leave the house. This will be a fun way to get them well-practiced at this, and it'll also show you what you need to work on with them. Make sure you actually go on a road trip, too. A fun day out will be a great reward.
- **Hide and Seek:** You might be surprised by how helpful this classic game is. If you show your kids where the really safe places in your house are, it'll help them think about safety if they need hiding places in the future. You'll have to make it seem like it's hard for you to find them, though!
- **Find the House!** My kids are too good at this to do it over short distances now, but the beauty of this is that you can make it harder as they get better at it. When you're out driving as a family, get your children to figure out the way back to the house. It's a fun challenge, and it helps them to practice their navigational skills.
- **Playing Doctor:** This is more for younger children who still enjoy playing doctor, but it's a great way for them to practice basic first-aid skills. Get out slings and bandages so they can treat their patients and improve their ability.

Talking to your family about the possibility of a nuclear threat may not be easy, but you're going to thank yourself if the worst ever happens. You don't want an emergency situation to arise and have to explain it all on the spot, wasting precious time and adding a ton of extra stress to the situation. Talking to your family is part of being prepared—and it's how you'll know that they're prepared to stay safe if something terrible happens—a scenario we'll look at in the next chapter.

6

MAYDAY! WHAT TO DO AS SOON AS YOU LEARN OF A NUCLEAR DISASTER

When the accident happened in Fukushima, residents only had a 10-minute warning of the tsunami. At that point, they had no idea of the nuclear danger that would follow or that nearly half a million people would have to leave their homes (BBC News 2023). Whether it's a natural disaster or a nuclear one, we're not going to have a lot of warning before it happens, and we'll need to act quickly as soon as we hear of a nuclear event. In this chapter, we're going to look at what will happen immediately and how you can take action as soon as you need to.

HEARING ABOUT THE DISASTER

If you're facing a nuclear strike rather than an accident, you're more likely to have some warning. The most likely scenario is that you'd get a Wireless Emergency Alert (WEA) in the form of a text message. This would also be broadcast on TVs and radios by the Emergency Alert System (EAS). There may even be a Presidential Alert issued by the White House, which would be sent to all cell phones throughout the country. Let's say the threat came from Russia. If it were to aim a nuclear-armed intercontinental ballistic missile at the States, we'd have no more than 30 minutes to find shelter; if the weapon was launched from a submarine closer to the country, we might have as little as 10 minutes warning (Bendix, McFall-Johnsen, and Barnes 2023). Even with the alerts in place, we're not going to have much time to take cover.

In the case of a nuclear accident, a warning would be issued as soon as an incident was discovered, but this wouldn't be in advance of it happening. Residents living within 10 miles of a nuclear plant are included in the Emergency Planning Zone and may receive alerts in the form of a siren, a radio alert, a WEA on their cell phone, or a prerecorded message from a public safety warning system (United States Nuclear Regulatory Commission 2024). If you hear a warning like this, find the Emergency Alert System for your region on your TV and radio, and follow any instructions given. If you're outside of the Emergency Planning Zone, however, you may not receive an alert. Your best course of action in this case is to stay indoors if you hear of a nuclear accident and tune into local media to hear what the official advice is (United States Nuclear Regulatory Commission 2024).

WHAT TO DO IMMEDIATELY

As we saw in earlier chapters, the minutes after a nuclear blast are the most critical. Your chances of radiation exposure are 55% lower an hour after the accident and 80% lower after a full 24 hours (John Hopkins Center for Health Security n.d.). Your immediate actions are, therefore, the ones that will make the most difference.

Get as far inside as you can, following the advice we discussed in Chapter 3, and cover your nose and mouth with a mask, handkerchief, or scarf until the fallout has finished (Monmouth County, N.J. n.d.). Remember to seal yourself inside, closing all doors and windows and taping up any openings into the outside world (such as chimneys and vents). If you're outside at the time of the explosion, get to the nearest safe place you can to shelter, avert your eyes from the flash of light, and keep your nose and mouth covered. You want to be safely sheltered before the fallout happens, which will come about 10 minutes after the explosion (International Commission on Radiological Protection n.d.).

During the first 24 hours, you have some chance of reducing your radiation exposure. If you were outside when it happened, shower with warm water as quickly as you can, applying soap gently so as not to break the protective barrier your skin gives you. If you don't have access to a shower, wash yourself as best you can with the resources you have. If you need to help others to do this (children or family members with disabilities, for example), wear gloves and a mask, and take steps to decontaminate yourself again afterward. You should also bathe any pets who were exposed, but if you can, try to do this in a separate room so that their hair doesn't contaminate anyone else. If you have any cuts, cover them before you take a shower, and avoid using lotions or creams, which can keep radioactive particles trapped in your hair and skin. There could also be debris caught in your nose, ears, and eyelids, so clean these and blow your nose. All the outer layers of clothing you were wearing should then be placed (along with any washcloths you've used) in a sealed plastic bag (Bendix, McFall-Johnsen, and Barnes 2023).

The recommendation is to stay in your shelter for 24 hours unless it becomes unsafe (e.g., the building collapses). Obviously, if this happens, you will need to self-evacuate, but otherwise, this is discouraged before safe routes out of the danger zone have been established (International Commission on Radiological Protection n.d.). Listen for emergency broadcasts so that you're up-to-date with the current advice.

After 24 hours have passed, the radiation levels outdoors will be much lower, but you may still need to protect yourself. Stay inside, keep listening to the advice, and make sure you're prepared to evacuate if it's required. It's likely that you'll be asked to evacuate within a week, but it may be that the advice is to stay in your shelter.

If you need to go outside for any reason during this time (such as to find a better shelter if yours has become dangerous), keep your mouth and nose covered, and, if you can, cover your clothes and shoes with plastic. Once you get back, this, along with your top layer of clothing and your shoes, should be removed, and you will need to shower again. Bear in mind that children and expectant mothers are the most vulnerable to radiation, so do your best to keep them inside (International Commission on Radiological Protection n.d.). Most of the fallout after a nuclear explosion will take around a week to settle on the ground, so you're still not safe to be outside unless it's absolutely necessary (Bendix, McFall-Johnsen, and Barnes 2023).

NAVIGATING THE IMMEDIATE ISSUES

With the protective measures taken, you're going to need to focus on survival during the time that you're sheltering and listening out for updates. Let's take a look at your primary concerns at this time.

Separation from Loved Ones

In an ideal world, your whole family would be together, but it may be that the emergency happens when children are in school and members of your family are at work or in the hospital. Rest assured that facilities like schools, care homes, and hospitals have emergency plans in place, and everyone will be taken care of as well as possible. I'm sure all of us will want to reunite as quickly as we can, but if you attempt this before it's safe, it could expose you all to radiation.

If you have the ability to text, do this to reach them rather than calling (the phone networks will be busy with emergencies), and pass on any reliable information you have about what's going on. Make sure you trust this information, though—there are bound to be unofficial sources that may not be imparting accurate advice (US Department of Homeland Security 2024).

I have no doubt that it will be extremely distressing to be away from your family, in particular your children, at this time, but the best thing you can do for everyone is stay put and trust that they're being taken care of until you're able to evacuate.

Food and Drink Safety Procedures

As we've discussed, all food, drink, and medication that's kept in a closed container inside your shelter will be safe. However, if the blast causes any damage to your house (like broken windows), it's possible that radioactive materials will get in and contaminate anything that isn't covered or packaged. Steer clear of these items, and wipe containers and packets down with soap and water before handling them (don't forget to seal any washcloths you use in plastic bags afterward). Throw away anything that doesn't look or smell right, including anything in your fridge or freezer, if the power goes out.

You already know that food and water outside will not be safe, and when it comes to water, your emergency supply will be the safest. Drinking tap water may or may not be safe—pay attention to the advice from the health and water departments and follow their guidance (US Department of Homeland Security 2024).

With medication, the same advice goes as it does for food, with one exception. If you have a life-sustaining medication that isn't in its packaging, the risk of taking it is less than the risk of not taking it. You may swallow a small amount of radioactive material, but if you need that medication to stay alive, it's worth taking the risk. The same is true if someone in your family is severely dehydrated and you've run out of your water supply. Start by using the water in the toilet cistern and hot water tank, but if this, too, runs out and you still don't have confirmation that tap water is safe to drink, it will be better for them to drink it than to risk death from dehydration (US Department of Homeland Security 2024). Just to be clear, even if your tap water has not been confirmed as safe, you can still use it for decontamination purposes.

Preparing to Evacuate

Unless you have no choice and your shelter is not safe, wait for the official guidance before you evacuate. A number of factors will be taken into consideration when evacuation routes and destinations are determined. Experts will be looking at the levels of radiation, the damage from the blast, and the weather, among other things, and this may look different in different areas. You may not even be instructed to evacuate. If you are, however, you will probably be asked to go to a specific place, which is likely to be a mass shelter. You'll also be given instructions about how to pick your children up from school or collect other family members from care facilities. If you have a pet, listen carefully for specific instructions for them. Some shelters will allow pets, while others only accept service animals (US Department of Homeland Security 2024).

Since you don't know what you'll be instructed to do, it's best to prepare for evacuation. Ideally, every member of your family will already have a bug-out bag ready to go. If this isn't the case, use the time in which you're sheltering to pack essential items—but don't leave the shelter in order to do this. Once you're instructed to leave, turn off your utilities and unplug any electrical equipment. I think it would be a good idea to leave a note to tell other people where your family has gone and when you left, too, along with a cell phone number. If you have pets in your group, make sure you bring a cage for them, along with all their necessary supplies, including a leash.

Bear in mind that you will not be able to return to your home until officials tell you it's safe to do so. You can't go back for anything you forget.

Medical Care

Immediately after a nuclear blast, there's a chance that someone in your family could be injured, either by the blast itself or by flying debris. They may also get burns or radiation injuries. Only people whose injuries are life-threatening should attempt to get professional medical care. Hospitals will be overwhelmed, and only the most serious injuries will be treated, so you'll need to do the best you can for any member of your party who's injured. Apply direct pressure to wounds with a clean gauze, cover the area to prevent infection, and wrap anyone who's been injured in a blanket so they stay warm. Cover burns lightly with a clean gauze, being careful not to use anything that could leave lint behind (this can increase the chances of infection), and remember not to use creams or ointments. Try to avert shock by lying the person down and elevating their feet by around 12 inches, keeping the burned area at a higher level than their head if you can. For serious burns covering large areas of the body, you'll need to call 911 or go to the nearest hospital to get help (US Department of Homeland Security 2024). Be sure to take safety precautions for yourself if you need to do this, and decontaminate yourself by removing your outer layers once you reach the hospital.

Detecting Radiation

Ionizing radiation can't be detected using our senses, so in order to check that your shelter is safe from it, you'll need equipment. We talked about the Geiger-Mueller counter in Chapter 4, but let's get a little more specific now (United States Nuclear Regulatory Commission 2020):

- **Personal Radiation Detector (PRD):** This is a small wearable device that detects neutron or gamma radiation and signals when radiation levels are high. This is usually shown on a scale of intensity, which means you can zone in on the source of radiation. This would be good if you had a piece of clothing that had been contaminated and was affecting the environment, but it isn't as sensitive as some of the other options, and it can't tell you exactly what it is that's responsible for the radiation.
- **Handheld Survey Meter:** This will measure how much radiation is in the space and display it in time (as counts per minute or second) or in levels of exposure to radiation per hour (as microroentgen (μR) or microrem (μrem)). The majority of handheld survey meters will detect only beta and gamma radiation, but high-end models will also detect alpha and neutron radiation.

- **Radiation Isotope Identification Device (RIID):** This will analyze the radiation's spectrum of energy, which means it can identify the exact material emitting radiation.

Radiation detector devices range wildly in price. For me, I think the biggest benefit would be to detect any contamination that has made it into the shelter so that this could be removed, minimizing the danger of exposure. I'm personally not sure it's worth spending a lot of money on this, though. There's some benefit in knowing if the danger is worse anywhere in the vicinity, but if you're already doing everything you can to protect yourself from radiation exposure, knowing exactly how high it is doesn't really help you and could just end up being an extra source of anxiety.

Keeping Children Calm

Everybody's going to be stressed and anxious in this situation, but these emotions are harder for kids because they have less understanding of what's going on and feel even less like they can control events than we do. They also don't have all the years of experience of facing stressful situations that we do, and younger children, especially, can't always communicate their emotions. They become even more vulnerable if they've already experienced trauma or have a developmental difference (CDC 2024).

Really, this is where the preparation work you've been doing with them well in advance of any disaster comes in. If your children know your emergency plans, they'll feel a greater sense of control over the situation, and they'll know roughly what they can expect to happen. It will also ease their minds to know how to approach emergency situations using the skills they don't necessarily need to use that much in their ordinary lives. None of this will help to reassure them if they're at school when disaster strikes, however. You can prepare them for this possibility, too, by finding out about the school's emergency plans and talking them through with your children.

If you are with your children when the crisis happens, you can help them by staying calm and doing your best to reassure them. Our kids are always looking to us as guides to the appropriate response in a situation, and if we're calm, they're more likely to follow suit. It's natural that you might find this difficult in this situation. If you're struggling, try to focus on your breathing. Diaphragmatic breathing may help you here—and it's something you can teach your children to do as well. Lay your hand over your stomach and breathe in deeply through your nose for five seconds before releasing your breath through your mouth for five seconds. Repeat this until you feel calmer.

You can also help your children by being open about what's happening and simplifying it as much as you need to in order for them to understand. We all feel less stressed when we feel like we know what's happening.

TAKE ACTION!

You've already built your emergency plan, but I think it's a good idea to also create a set of guidelines taking you through the main things you'll need to do as soon as you hear of a nuclear disaster. These aren't familiar routines, and the mind has a tendency to go blank when panic sets in. I have a "Nuclear Protocol" checklist that I keep with my emergency supplies, and it gives me peace of mind to know that I won't need to remember anything when it's all kicking off.

Here's what you might include in it:

- **At First Alert:**
    - Cover your nose and mouth
    - Don't look at the blast!
    - Get as far inside as you can
    - Seal all openings to the outside world
- **First 24 hours:**
    - Remove the outer layer of clothing and seal it in a polythene bag
    - Shower with warm water and soap
    - Blow nose and clean ears and eyelids
    - Wear PPE if you need to help others
    - Bathe animals
    - Seal used washcloths in polythene bags
    - Listen for emergency broadcasts
    - Prepare to evacuate

Unless you're advised to evacuate, you're probably going to be bugging in for a little longer than this, but eventually, you may be required to move. The world may look very different at this point. In the next chapter, we'll look at how you can get through this, whatever it may look like.

7

STAY ALERT—SURVIVAL FOR THE FIRST FEW MONTHS

We can really only draw on what's happened in the past with other nuclear disasters; we can't know for sure how it might look the next time—particularly if the next time turns out to be a nuclear war. In this chapter, we'll look at survival, both when you have to stay in place and when you have to evacuate. It's quite likely that you'll need to do both in the first few months after a nuclear event.

SHELTERING IN PLACE

Remember that you're going to be staying inside for at least 24 hours (unless you're directed otherwise). This could go on for a month or more, though, and if this happens, you'll need to take extra care of your family's emotional and physical well-being.

Keeping up to date with alerts and local news will help you with this—it will give you a sense of stability at a very uncertain time. Make sure that you're only relying on credible sources, though, and be mindful not to stay focused on endless news cycles that could end up making you more anxious. Be mindful of the emotional experiences of everyone sheltering with you; they may need your help to find their way through.

Your physical health is important, too. Eat regularly, maintain a sleep schedule, and do as much exercise within the shelter as possible. This will obviously be limited, but there are always things you can do to keep your blood flowing and your joints from stiffening up.

A Word About Your Supplies

For as long as you need to stay inside, you need to be prepared to survive, and this means considering your supplies. I would assume that this is something you've already thought about in detail now that you're reading a book about nuclear survival specifically. If you haven't, I'd advise you to read my other books to make sure you cover all your bases fully.

The amount of food families tend to store for an emergency varies. Some very committed preppers will tell you that they have supplies to last them 10 years. Personally, I think aiming for three months is sufficient to cover most short-term disasters; for ones that could go on for longer, you can supplement with your survival skills and knowledge of the resources available to you. It's also much more realistic if you don't have a huge storage space in which you can keep your supplies. For food stocks, I'll again refer you to *The Prepper's Pantry*, but you'll also need water, backup power and heating/light sources, toiletries, medications, and specific survival items, for which I'd refer you to *When Crisis Hits Suburbia* and *Prepare Your Home for a Sudden Grid-Down Situation*.

Even if you're not prepping to survive only on your own supplies for 10 years, you'll still need space to keep all of your resources. If you have a basement, this would be ideal (and it will also be the best place to shelter in the event of a nuclear accident). I do realize, though, that this isn't possible for everyone. Being as prepared as *you* can be is your best course of action—no matter how limited you might perceive that to be.

Food and Water Safety

We've talked a bit about food and water safety, but I think it's worth the reminder. If a nuclear emergency occurs, we're going to be in a very different situation from any we've ever been in before, and the more firmly we have this safety information in the backs of our minds, the better.

Remember, in any radiation emergency, you should only consume food that's sealed inside containers or within the protection of your fridge, freezer, or a closed cupboard or pantry. You can also eat food in sealed containers that were kept outside, as long as you have wiped them thoroughly before opening them.

If you're sheltering somewhere in your home that gives you access to your kitchen facilities, make sure that you wipe down anything you use (including utensils and countertops). Any cloths you use for decontamination should then be discarded in a sealed bag or container, and you should always wash your hands thoroughly afterward. All of this advice goes for feeding your pets, too. Remember, you can't eat anything from outside until there's official confirmation that it's safe.

If you have an infant to feed, the recommendation is to prepare baby formula using bottled water or to use a pre-made formula. Breastfeeding mothers should be safe to continue feeding as long as they haven't been exposed to radiation; if they have, they should use formula or milk that they've previously expressed until they've been medically assessed. If this is not possible, however, they will need to continue breastfeeding because the risk to the baby without this will be greater than the risk of radiation exposure (Burch 2023).

Tap water is safe for you to use for cleaning and decontamination, but avoid cooking with it or drinking it (unless absolutely necessary) until it has been confirmed as safe. Drinks you have in sealed containers or that are protected by your fridge and freezer are also safe. Again, wipe everything down with a regular household cleaner or soap and water first, and dispose of the cleaning cloth securely.

Getting the Most from Your Supplies

If you're sheltering at home with no real idea for how long, you want to make sure that your supplies last for as long as possible, and this means thinking carefully about the order in which you use them. Start with the food in your fridge because it will be the most perishable. Only head to the freezer and the pantry once your most perishable supplies have been used up (unless the power is out, in which case you'll need to use your frozen food quickly). Be aware, though, that you don't need to get rid of food just because it's past its expiration date. I wouldn't take the chance with animal products or rusted or swollen cans, but for anything else, you can make your decision based on the smell and appearance of the food. Remember that if you need to cook anything, you'll need to decontaminate all your equipment first.

If you need to shelter in place for an extended period of time, you want to consider how you can produce your own food without going outside, where contamination is a serious risk. This will serve you afterward, too. Even if you eventually have to find somewhere new to live, you may not be far enough away from the area to grow food outdoors safely. This is why I'm working on my indoor gardening skills, and I'd suggest that you do the same. Get those microgreens growing!

EVACUATION

Remember that evacuation alerts will come through the radio and television, as well as through alerts to your phone. Pay attention to these, and be ready to go as soon as you're directed. Make sure everyone in your party has a bug-out bag ready to go and knows exactly where it is. There's always a chance that you'll be left to fend for yourself, but this is highly unlikely. Everyone in your neighborhood will also be evacuated, and there will almost certainly be a plan set into motion to get you all to safety. That said, I think it would be worth having a backup evacuation plan that takes you as far away from the site as possible, just in case something happens to prevent official plans from being instigated. You can read more about what to think about when you're planning an evacuation location in *The*

Bug-Out Book. This is also where you'll find comprehensive guidance for putting together a bug-out bag, but to give you a brief overview, these are the sorts of items you'll need to consider (Bug Out Bag Academy 2024):

- Drinking water (3 liters per person)
- Water bottle
- Water purification methods and filters
- Energy bars
- Dehydrated meals
- Cooking equipment (including stove)
- Lightweight but warm clothing (think in layers!)
- Raincoat
- Sleeping bag and blankets
- Tinder and lighter
- First aid kit
- Survival blanket
- Personal hygiene supplies
- Towel
- Survival knife
- Multi-tool
- Flashlight and candles
- Batteries and power banks
- Communication devices
- Cash (I'd recommend about several hundred dollars in small bills)
- Important documents
- Map and compass
- Notepad and pencil
- Whistle

- Rope
- Duct tape
- Face masks
- Trash bags
- Resealable baggies
- Sewing kit

Although you'll most likely be given instructions about where to evacuate to and how, it's impossible to know what resources you'll have access to, which is why your bug-out bag is so important.

Once it's time to leave, try to let someone out-of-state know where you're going, and do your best to secure your home, locking all doors and windows just as you would if you were going on vacation. Unplug all your electronics and shut off the utilities. Only take the evacuation routes that have been recommended—experts have analyzed the area and will have a far better idea of the safest options than you do. Remember, too, that you should not come home until you're told by officials that it's safe to do so.

MANAGING THE PSYCHOLOGICAL IMPACT

As we've discussed, any member of your family could be anxious, scared, or upset by what's happened, and it's likely that all of you will be a little quicker to irritate than usual. The psychological impact could be much greater than this, though.

You may notice changes in your thoughts or behavior patterns (or those of other family members). You might have flashbacks to the blast, which could then lead to physical responses like a racing heart. You may find it difficult to eat or sleep, your ability to concentrate may be impacted, and you may experience physical symptoms of stress like headaches, chest pain, and nausea (American Psychological Association 2013). You may also struggle to lift your mood. This is why building your mental resilience in advance is so important, but don't beat yourself up if you experience disaster-related stress even after having done this.

I may be thoroughly prepared for disaster, but I've been lucky so far. I've never experienced the trauma that comes with this, so I can't speak from my own experience. However, we can follow official guidance given to people in these situations (US Department of Homeland Security 2024):

- Talk openly about your emotions.
- Avoid holding yourself responsible for any part of your family's situation. You did your best, and this was not something you could control.
- Take care of your health as best you can under the circumstances by trying to eat as healthily as you can, resting regularly, exercising, and relaxing your mind.
- Try to establish a temporary routine with your family.

In all likelihood, your biggest concern at this time will be your children, who may be very scared or sad. Younger children might revert to behavior patterns they'd had earlier in life, such as demonstrating separation anxiety or wetting the bed; older kids might become angry or distressed. You can make the situation less distressing for them by staying calm and trying to manage your own feelings, as well as letting them know they can talk to you about theirs. You may also find that, if they do this, you'll be able to answer questions and address any misconceptions they have, which could make a big difference in setting their mind at ease. Don't neglect physical contact, either. I know I'm guilty of this sometimes if I'm feeling stressed out myself, but our kids need us to hug them and reassure them physically as well as with our words.

The US Department of Homeland Security has outlined common reactions to a disaster by age. These don't relate directly to a nuclear disaster, but they do give us some idea of how our children might react in this situation (US Department of Homeland Security 2024):

- **0-2 Years:** They can't describe how they're feeling or what has happened, but they are capable of remembering sensory information, which you may see evidence of later through their reactions to triggers. At this age, they may be more irritable or clingy, and they might cry more than they usually do.
- **3-6 Years:** Children this age often feel helpless in the face of disaster. They can't protect themselves, and they're aware of this, which often makes them scared and insecure, and you may find that they're particularly anxious about being separated from you and your partner.
- **7-10 Years:** At this age, children understand more about what's going on, and they may become very

preoccupied with it. You could see a whole array of reactions, ranging from sadness and fear to anger.
- **11-18 Years:** Their understanding is more sophisticated now, which means that their responses are more likely to be similar to your own. They may feel intense emotions that they don't know how to talk about with you, however, so remember to check in with them, even if they seem like they're doing ok.

TAKE ACTION!

Ideally, you already have food stored in preparation for a disaster, and if you haven't, I'd really recommend reading up on this in more detail. However, I'd like to leave you with a step-by-step plan for putting this together quickly. Take action on this, and you'll know that, eventually, you'll be able to feed your family for at least three months.

1. **Work out your budget.** You still have to survive now, so don't spend more on stocking up than you can realistically afford. Be savvy about your shopping when you get to that stage—you'll almost certainly be able to extend your budget if you shop around a bit and look for offers.
2. **Organize, acquire, and rotate your supplies.** Start by deciding what you need and where you're going to store it. Then, you can start building up your stocks by preserving your own food and shopping for supplies. Once you have these in place, you'll need to use them and replace them as necessary, starting with the oldest

ones first. This means nothing will turn bad, and nothing will be forgotten.

3. **Use the space you have.** This is why organization is so important before you even start acquiring your supplies: You need to have this in mind as soon as you start storing food. Ideally, you'll have a basement or a pantry you can use, but I'm well aware that these are luxuries not everyone has. Be creative about it! The tops of cupboards, the spaces under beds, and the corners of little-used rooms are all fair game.

4. **Take your time.** As much as you may want to build up your stockpile quickly, you can probably afford to take it slow. This will allow you to spread out your expenses and take advantage of offers. One easy way to start adding to your pile is to buy two of every long-life item every time you're going to buy one anyway. You can use one and store the other.

5. **Set up a replenishable food source that you can tend to indoors.** Now is the time to invest in indoor gardening equipment and start developing this skill, as we discussed in Chapter 4.

If you're evacuated, you'll only be allowed to go back home if experts are confident that the area has been decontaminated. In the next chapter, we'll look at survival in a new location if going home isn't advisable, as well as the precautions you can take if you are allowed back home.

8

THE NEW NORMAL—STRATEGIES FOR LONG-TERM SURVIVAL

The last nuclear disaster was Fukushima in 2011. To this day, some of the residents have not returned, even though the evacuation order was lifted in 2022, and some residents were permitted to return as early as 2016 (Jozuka and Yeung 2022). Case studies were conducted on three residents, all of whom had unrelated health concerns, and their reasons for not returning had to do with the healthcare they could access in the places they'd been evacuated to (Ito et al. 2023). This illustrates that the infrastructure of the areas had still not returned to normal 12 years later.

Although Fukushima was quite some time ago, it's the most recent example we have to draw on to figure out what life might look like in the aftermath of a nuclear disaster. The people who were evacuated from Tomioka, a town in Fukushima, found that their homes were separated into three categories: "in preparation to return," "return for short periods," and "never to return." These categories seemed somewhat arbitrary, and for those whose homes fell into the "never to return" category, the compensation from the government was only to go on for a limited amount of time. Many people struggled to afford a fresh start, and those who could go back were unclear about whether it was truly safe to do so. Cycles of shelters and temporary housing continued for many residents, leaving them unclear on their next move. A lot of families felt safer starting life somewhere new, but this wasn't made easy by the level of financial support given (Kim 2015).

What this tells us is that we can't guarantee anything. There may be some support available in the event of a nuclear disaster, but we don't know that this would be enough, and we don't know whether we'd ever be able to return home. There's every reason to be prepared to survive with limited support.

COULD YOU GO HOME?

Government guidance about responding to a nuclear detonation includes the recommendation that the affected area be divided into "damage zones," similar to the categories used after Fukushima, to guide emergency response teams. The outermost areas, where injuries are easy to address and damage to property is minimal, will be classed as a "light damage zone." In the "moderate damage zone," there will be significant damage to buildings and utilities, multiple fires, and more serious injuries. The "severe damage zone" will cover the area closest to the blast, where buildings have collapsed completely and radiation levels are high. The chances are, if you live in this zone, you probably won't survive; if you're lucky enough to get out, the possibility of ever returning home is very slim (Wolfson and Dalnoki-Veress 2022).

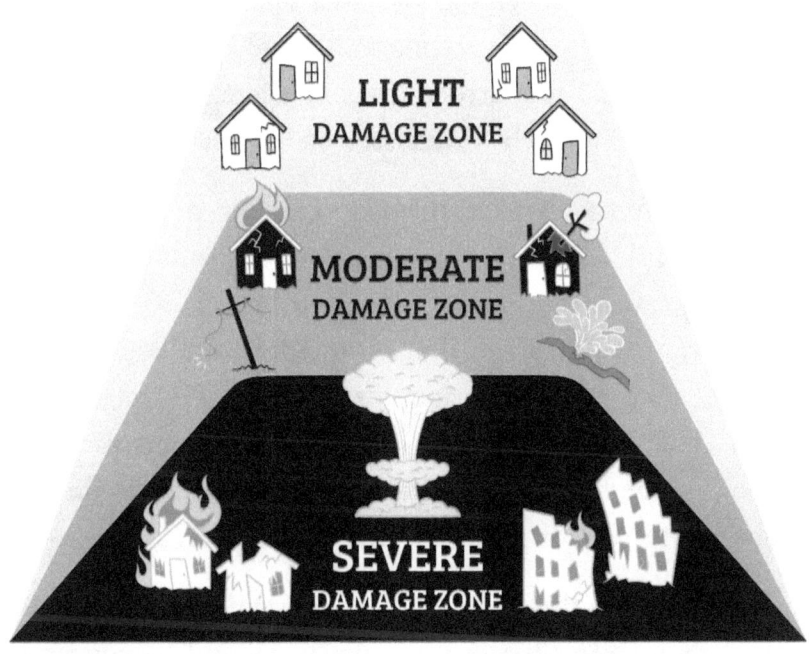

If you are able to go home, remember that this will not be permitted until officials are sure that it's safe, so your first action is to keep listening to advice and take steps only when you've been given the all-clear. If you're allowed to go home, the chances are that life isn't going to look the same as it did before you left. You may be facing restrictions, and you could still be exposed to health risks. You may find that you'd prefer *not* to go home. Indeed, studies of the consequences of nuclear power plant accidents have shown that people tend to be more fearful of the risks associated with going back than authorities anticipate, choosing not to return to a decontaminated area if it can't be used freely or if it feels uncomfortable. Some people are still concerned about radiation, even after reassurances of safety, prompting them to decide against returning. Residents who have an attachment to the area due to work, personal interests, or investments are more likely to return unless they believe that their property value will decrease—and let's be honest, this is very likely (Rasmussen and Wikström 2022).

After Fukushima, many residents were forced to stay away because their localities were too unsafe to return to (Kim 2015), and as we saw earlier, many never returned. In 2016, evacuation orders for Katsurao's Noyuki district were largely lifted, but only four households (out of a total of 30) planned to return. This was largely due to a concern about radiation, although some had simply settled elsewhere while decontamination efforts were in progress (Jozuka and Yeung 2022).

In a situation like this, once it is deemed safe to return, you will have a choice—and the chances are, you'll still be concerned about your safety if you do go home. Your decision will also depend on the type of nuclear disaster and exactly what damage has been done. If you and your family have survived by this point, and your home has survived too, even if radiation levels are safe, the infrastructure may have collapsed, and supply chains could be disrupted (Article 36 2015). Recovery may take some time. If you do decide to return under these circumstances, your supplies at home will be crucial, which is another good reason to stock for three months if you can.

FOOD PRODUCTION

The land around the Chornobyl nuclear reactor has only recently been deemed safe for food production almost four decades after the disaster (Bradley 2024). In the event of a similar accident, even if you were allowed to return home, it may be that you would be unable to grow your own food or even obtain local produce. However, if you live further away, you may be given the all-clear to return to your garden. If this happens, your first step is to thoroughly clean all of your gardening tools and prepare your soil, as we discussed in Chapter 4. You'll have to be patient and wait for the cover crop to grow, but the process will eventually allow you to grow safe crops (Survival Garden Seeds 2022).

This, however, is far less likely to be effective in the event of a nuclear war. If the two countries with the largest nuclear inventory (the US and Russia) were to engage in nuclear combat, over 165 million tons of soot would be sent into the upper atmosphere, reducing the level of natural light to under 40% of what we know now close to the equator and under 5% near the North and South Poles. There would be significantly less rain, and freezing conditions would prevail even in temperate areas, and this new climate could continue for 15 years (Benoit 2022). The result of this would be global crop failure for several years, with more chance of successful food production nearer to the equator (Mulhollem 2022).

In the case where you can eventually grow your own crops and in the case where growing food outdoors is next to impossible, a seed bank could be a potential asset. It means you'll have a variety of seeds, and while you won't be able to grow everything indoors, there is some hope of producing something. There are several options on the market, so it's worth taking your time to think about the most appropriate choice. I think it would still be worth choosing a seed bank that fits your growing zone, even if the climate does change dramatically. This situation may not happen, and you want something that will serve you in any disaster situation. You also want to make sure that the seeds included in it have a reasonable shelf life (which you may be able to extend by freezing them). A simple seed bank for one or two people can cost anything from $40 to $200, so work within your means, but make sure it contains enough seeds to sustain your family if you need to use it (Adamant 2018).

In the event of a global nuclear disaster (i.e., nuclear war), a seed bank probably wouldn't help you that much. Here, we need to rely on researchers. In a 2022 study, researchers from the Royal Swedish Academy of Sciences reflected on foods that may be able to withstand a nuclear disaster and be cultivated in the aftermath (Winstead and Jacobson 2022). This includes cassava, mopane worms, wild oyster mushrooms, wild spinach, oil palms, and baobab, among other wild edible foods, but the problem is that this may not be enough to sustain all survivors until food can be grown again (Gonçalves 2022).

Seaweed is also thought to have promise as a food source during a nuclear winter. Researchers have found that it could replace 45% of the planet's food in between nine and 14 months and would grow in abundance after a nuclear war (Jehn et al. 2024).

David Denkenberger, who runs Alliance to Feed the Earth in Disasters (ALLFED), believes that harvesting foods like seaweed and mushrooms could give us part of what we need for around three years, but he warns that a diet as restrictive as this would make us vulnerable to disease. He suggests that there are a few technological approaches we could use to grow food, including using the atmosphere's natural gas to produce protein and growing in greenhouses near the equator (Bendix 2020).

I find it comforting that researchers are looking into this, but it still doesn't give us much control—and this is where having a long-term emergency food supply, assuming your storage space remains intact after the disaster, would be a huge asset. I know I've recommended preparing for three months, but if you want to be thoroughly prepared (and this is a realistic option for you), up to four years' worth of food for your whole family would be ideal if this post-apocalyptic scene were to play out (Adamant 2018).

You should also be able to keep growing your microgreens and vegetables that are tolerant to shade inside, so there's another argument for taking up indoor gardening. There's a story coming out of the UK that makes this look hopeful, too. There are World War II tunnels beneath London that are being used as an urban farm called Growing Underground (GU). In an area spanning 6,000 square feet, over 100 tons of produce is grown each year, including broccoli, arugula, fennel, and salad leaves

(Kemp 2020). This is done with recycled water and LED heating—and without the use of soil (McDonagh 2021). It gives me hope that we *would* be able to produce some fresh food indoors, even in a nuclear winter.

WATER

Eventually, your supplies of bottled water will run out, and the water saved in your toilet cistern and hot water tank is finite, so finding safe drinking water will, at some point, become a priority. You can't remove radioactive contaminates by boiling the water, and standard home water filters won't do the job either. You can prepare for this situation, though.

Research has shown that distillers are able to remove uranium from water, which would remove alpha, beta, and gamma radiation (Muehling 2011). These are widely available commercially, so you could boost your preparation efforts by investing in one of these now.

You also have a few other options. Reverse osmosis is thought to be one of the most effective methods of decontaminating water affected by radioactive particles. Water is forced through a membrane containing extremely small pores, which allow water to pass through without taking the radioactive particles with it. Another option is ion exchange, in which water is passed through a resin containing exchangeable ions, which bond to the water more strongly than radioactive particles. As a result, the radioactive contaminants remain in the resin, and the safe exchangeable ions pass through. You can also use carbon filtration, which removes radioactive particles by absorbing the contaminates. With this method, the carbon must be replaced at a certain point because it will no longer be able to absorb the problematic materials (Taylor 2021).

You'll never be able to eliminate 100% of the radioactive contaminants in water, but you could take out a lot, and if you combined all these methods, you'd be able to remove even more (Taylor 2021). Equipment for all of these processes is commercially available for a few hundred dollars.

SOCIAL ASPECTS

To an extent, we have to speculate when we consider what kind of world we might be living in after a nuclear disaster, but what we can be fairly certain of is that you won't be the only family living in it. This means you're going to need to have ways to communicate, and you're going to need to stay safe.

Communication

Although it depends on the nature of the incident and how large an area is affected, it's quite likely that the power grid will be down, and it could take some time to get back up and running again. This means your communication devices are going to be important. All of the alternative communication methods we discussed in Chapter 4 may be as important in the long term as they are in the immediate aftermath of the disaster, and ideally, you'll have a few different options in case one fails.

We must also be aware of the EMP here, though, which will happen the moment a nuclear device is detonated. This can damage electronic devices that haven't been protected (Radiation Emergency Medical Management 2025). Unless you were very close to ground zero, your devices will probably be safe, but you can protect against this possibility by making a DIY Faraday cage (an enclosure that blocks electromagnetic fields) by wrapping a layer of cloth followed by three layers of tinfoil around your electronic equipment (make sure there aren't any gaps). You could also place your devices in a lidded steel garbage can lined with cloth (Underwater Kinetics 2023).

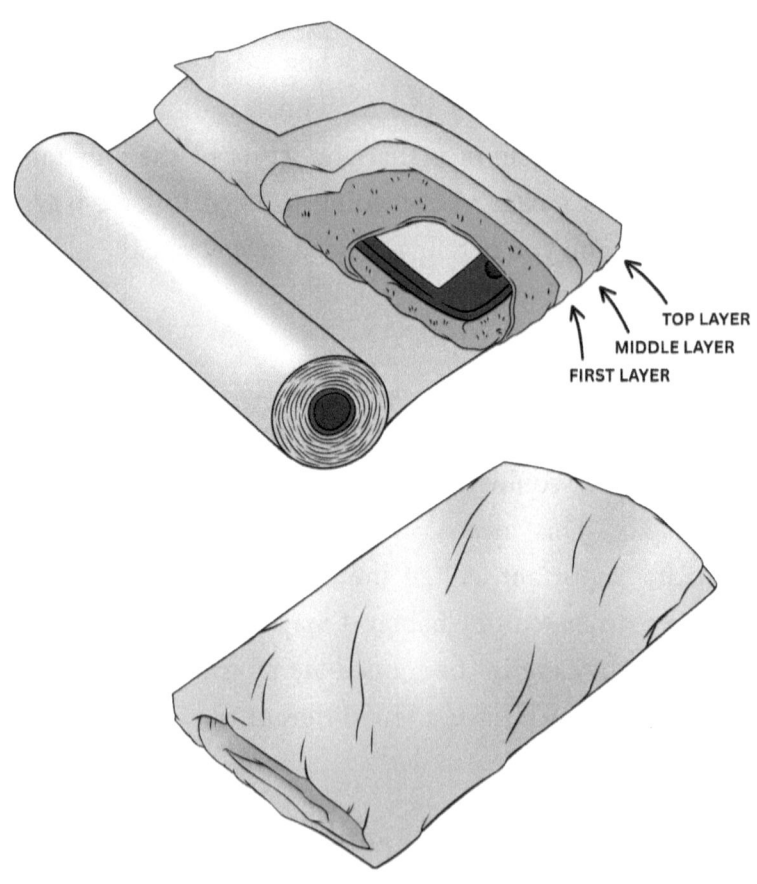

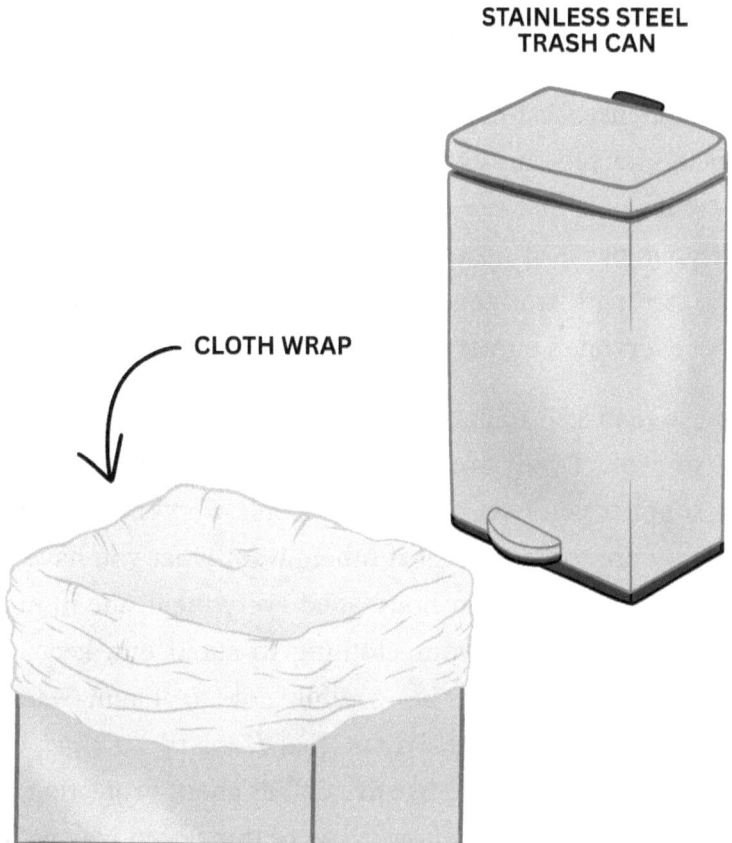

Defense

We have no evidence that a nuclear disaster would result in civilian violence, but it's a desperate situation, and people are unpredictable. It's a good idea to be prepared to defend yourself, and, again, the preparation you've already been doing will serve you well here. I would add, though, that self-defense isn't just about protecting yourself physically; it's also about being able to deal with anything that compromises your safety.

As well as the basic self-defense moves we discussed earlier, you'll need to work on your mental preparedness and your situational awareness, which is always going to be your first line of defense. You need to be aware of your surroundings in order to intercept any danger—those self-defense moves will be useless if you don't see a threat until it's upon you. You also want your physical fitness to be in top shape. In my opinion, cardio, strength training, and flexibility exercises should be a part of everyone's efforts to be prepared.

If you've managed to make it home, you may also want to take steps to protect your property. I'd start by keeping quiet about what supplies you have—the more people who know, the more likely you are to be a target if others want what you have. The next step is to make your house (and everyone inside it) inconspicuous. Don't allow your clothing to stand out, keep your windows covered, and be careful not to flaunt valuable resources. I'd refer you to *Prepare Your Home for a Sudden Grid-Down Situation* for comprehensive details about protecting your property, but here's a brief overview of things you may want to think about (Alexa R, Tactical.com 2021):

- Creating a secure perimeter around your house
- Using thick shrubs and trees for privacy (but be careful that they don't prevent you from seeing intruders)
- Using motion lights and cameras (if you're able to power them)
- Reinforcing your windows and doors with deadbolt locks, long screws, and window locks and bars

- Designating a safe room equipped with survival supplies (you could use your fallout room for this)

PSYCHOLOGICAL HEALTH

The psychological health of your family should be a priority after any kind of nuclear disaster, even if it isn't war-related. After Fukushima, there were many instances of post-traumatic stress disorder, anxiety, and depression, and this is consistent with the findings after non-nuclear disasters (Hori 2020). Psychological distress was also found to be higher in evacuees who had to relocate to an area outside Fukushima than in those who returned home (Harigane 2021).

The aftermath of a nuclear war could be even more complex. If we look at data collected after the Hiroshima and Nagasaki bombings, we can see that many people suffered from severe anxiety, psychic numbing, and disorganized behavior. Years later, survivors were affected by a variety of psychosomatic symptoms and survivor guilt (Salter 2001). We can expect to see similar effects in the event of a nuclear war, but we have a slight advantage now. There was less understanding of trauma in 1945 Japan than there is now, despite the treatment of psychological wounds like shell shock (Jones 2023).

Nonetheless, many survivors in today's world are likely to suffer from "disaster syndrome," which manifests as depression or anxiety to varying degrees of severity. As society is rebuilt, we may see more anger and blame come into play, which could lead to hostility and violence (Young 2019). Being aware of these possibilities is the first way to protect yourself, as you're more likely to recognize changes in your own thoughts and behavior or in those of your family. You can also take proactive steps to take care of your mental health, both in anticipation of disaster syndrome and as a response to it.

I think self-awareness is the key here. Think about how your behavior changes if you perceive a threat. There are several versions of you that influence your reactions. These can be described as your "overwhelmed self," your "adult self," and your "survival self"(Schwartz and Pines 2020). Your overwhelmed self is childlike and vulnerable, while your adult self is much more capable and can reassure your overwhelmed self.

Unfortunately, it's not usually either of these two characters who are running the show when you feel threatened: It's usually your survival self, the self that's impulsive, reactive, and not always that logical. When you're in survival mode, you're able to see little more than the threat, and your pre-frontal cortex shuts down, causing you to react before thinking about what you're doing. This is great for staying focused on the immediate issue, but it's not so good for solving complex problems (Schwartz and Pines 2020).

If you're able to pay attention to your emotions and observe them rather than letting them take over, you're able to get a little distance. You can amplify this by calming yourself using breathing techniques, and this should enable you to reflect on the situation more calmly, stepping into your adult self, who can make sense of the situation and reassure you. Essentially, this is self-soothing, and it's just as important to adults as it is to children.

If you catch yourself thinking in extremes, dwelling on negative points, or leaping to conclusions without weighing up the evidence, it's likely that your thoughts are distorting and fueling your fear. The good news is that if you're aware of this, you can do something about it (Swinton 2020):

- Identify the negative thought that's making you anxious.
- Look carefully at the evidence and find a fact that supports a more positive outlook.
- Consider the rational advice you might give to a friend experiencing the same fear.
- Talk to other people to make sure you're seeing the situation objectively.
- Turn your focus to finding solutions rather than focusing on the problem itself.

None of this is to say that there isn't a very good reason for fear, anxiety, and negative thought patterns at a time like this. However, they're not helpful to survival, and if you're able to overcome them, even for a moment, you have a much better chance of solving problems as they happen and managing your overall mental health.

All the self-care you're able to afford yourself in this situation will help, too. While it's true that the world may look very different and some things may not be possible, it's worth reminding yourself of the things that keep your mental health in good shape during non-traumatic times (National Institute of Mental Health 2024):

- Exercise regularly.
- Hydrate and eat a balanced diet.
- Decrease your consumption of alcohol and caffeine.
- Prioritize sleep.
- Engage in relaxing activities like meditation, reading, and breathing exercises.
- Organize tasks according to priority.
- Practice gratitude for the things you still have.
- Talk to the people around you.

TAKE ACTION!

Take some time to create an emergency self-care kit to add to your bug-out bag. This might seem a little silly to you right now, but I can't over-emphasize the importance of taking care of your mental health. Keep your self-care kit light and space-saving, and you may well thank yourself later. You can include anything that you feel may soothe you in a high-stress situation, but just in case you're stuck, here are a few ideas that might help you:

- Adult coloring books and pencils
- A book of positive affirmations
- A stress ball
- A journal and pen
- Essential oil with a relaxing scent (e.g., lavender)

- A book of puzzles
- A comforting item (like a childhood toy)

Your health, both psychological and physical, is the most important thing to protect in the aftermath of a nuclear disaster, and we'll keep our focus on this in the next chapter.

PRIORITY #1—PROTECTING YOUR HEALTH IN A POST-NUCLEAR WORLD

In Chapter 2, we looked at the health risks associated with a nuclear accident, the severity of which depends on the level of radiation to which you're exposed. The higher the dose of radiation you receive, the more likely it is that you'll experience adverse consequences. The body is able to repair itself if the dose is low, so if you've managed to stay protected, you may be able to get away with minimal negative effects (World Health Organization 2023). In this chapter, we'll look at how you can protect your health, both in the immediate aftermath of a disaster and further down the line.

RADIATION SICKNESS

When you have prolonged or extreme exposure to ionizing radiation, you run the risk of developing radiation sickness or acute radiation syndrome (ARS). This can be life-threatening, and it can take one of three main forms: Cerebrovascular syndrome (which affects the flow of blood to the brain and occurs after the whole body has been exposed to an extremely high dose of radiation), gastrointestinal syndrome (which affects your digestive system), and hematopoietic syndrome (which affects the formation of the blood cells). The severity of the symptoms depends on the amount of radiation the body absorbs (Cleveland Clinic 2024).

The first signs of radiation sickness are generally nausea and vomiting, and they give you a clue as to how much radiation a person has been exposed to. If these symptoms don't surface for weeks, it's an indication that the exposure was mild. If, however, they appear immediately or within a few days, you can assume that the exposure was high (Mayo Clinic 2024). These are the other symptoms that may indicate radiation sickness (Medicine Plus 2023):

- Weakness or fatigue
- Confusion
- Bleeding from the mouth or nose
- Bloody stool or diarrhea
- Hair loss
- Fever
- Dehydration
- Inflammation of exposed body parts
- Ulcers
- Low blood pressure

Once these symptoms present themselves, radiation sickness follows three stages (Cleveland Clinic 2024):

- **Prodromal Stage:** The early symptoms discussed above
- **Latent Asymptomatic Stage:** A period in which no symptoms present, usually occurring from anything from a few hours to 21 days after exposure
- **Systemic Illness Stage:** Changes in the body and worsening symptoms, usually within 60 days of exposure

As we discussed earlier, it is possible to give first aid to people suffering from radiation poisoning, but you run the risk of exposing yourself to radiation if you do so. Remember to decontaminate them and protect yourself if you find yourself in this situation, and if it's possible to call the emergency services or get the patient to a hospital, do so.

The approach to treating radiation sickness depends on its severity, but it always begins with decontamination. Sometimes surgical procedures are necessary; at other times, supportive care (like replenishing fluids and administering medication) is enough. Where it's feasible, psychotherapy is arranged (Cleveland Clinic 2024). However, were we to find ourselves amid an all-out nuclear war, these treatments may not be available due to shortages of medical staff, equipment, and facilities.

Potassium Iodide

Potassium iodide is available over the counter right now, but it will only be prescribed within the Emergency Planning Zone if a disaster strikes. This is because the risk of exposure is much higher in this area. Furthermore, it's prescribed only to a limited group of people because the risk of side effects increases with age. There's also less risk of thyroid cancer caused by radiation in people over the age of 40 (World Health Organization 2023).

If you do stock it, it's worth knowing that potassium iodide tablets don't decrease in effectiveness with time, and it's safe to take them if they're past their expiration date (United States Nuclear Regulatory Committee 2024). I've heard it asked whether iodized table salt would work to protect the thyroid after radiation exposure. The answer to this is no: It doesn't contain a high enough concentration of iodine, and eating a large amount of iodized salt wouldn't do your health any favors.

SHORT TERM SAFETY

One of the most important things you can do to keep yourself safe in the short term is to protect yourself as best you can. This means sheltering inside until the fallout is over and using PPE when handling anything that may have been contaminated or dealing with someone who's been exposed to radiation.

Beyond this, your medical supplies need to be solid. In the case of an accident at a nuclear power plant, because only a small proportion of the population would be affected, medical treatment would probably be available. Even if there were staff, medicine, or hospital bed shortages, it's likely that everything could be sourced from elsewhere, or patients could be sent to neighboring hospitals. However, in the event of a nuclear war, there could be a real problem with supply and demand in the healthcare sector. Analysis in the 1980s pointed out that the large cities that are likely to be targeted in an attack are also where most of the medical resources are (Abrams 1986). This is still the case today, and this could mean that there simply aren't enough resources to treat everyone who would need it. This would make your own resources very precious.

NUTRITION

With a carefully built emergency supply, you should be able to maintain a healthy diet for at least the first few months following a nuclear incident, but you're going to fare far better if your diet is healthy now. A balanced and nutritious diet will protect you against diseases like diabetes and heart disease, and it will keep your immune system in good shape. There's obviously a lot of depth we could go into about exactly what a balanced diet looks like, but to keep it simple, your diet should consist of a wide variety of natural whole foods, including staple items like potatoes, rice, and cereals, fruits and vegetables, meat and dairy products (or vegetarian/vegan alternatives), and legumes like beans and lentils. Oils and fats have an important role in the diet, but it's best to minimize your consumption of saturated and trans fats, which can increase the risk of health problems. Sugar and salt, too, should be limited (World Health Organization n.d.).

When it comes to your emergency supply, ensuring your family can maintain a balanced diet throughout the crisis should be a high priority. Make sure you stock up on a range of foods from different food groups, aiming to cover a full spectrum of vitamins and minerals across your supplies.

We touched briefly on ways to preserve food in Chapter 4, but I'd like to make the case for freeze-dried food in particular. It maintains its quality for up to 30 years, which means all its nutrients stay intact (Adamant 2021). You can sometimes find freeze-dried food in the grocery store, but the quality does vary depending on the quality of the food in the first place. If you grow your own food, though, it's a great way to preserve both the flavor and the nutritional value, and you can buy home freeze-dryers to make the process easier. They're quite an investment (they tend to start at around $2,000), but I think they quickly prove their value.

If you're starting your prepper's pantry from scratch and you're looking for a quick and easy route, you can get prepper food kits that will feed a family for a year. These contain freeze-dried foods, among other long-life products (Haynes 2018). This is definitely an option, but it isn't the most cost-effective one. A better approach would be to build your stockpile gradually, adding items to your weekly grocery list and stashing them away until you have a supply that will last you in a crisis.

Again, I'd refer you to *The Prepper's Pantry* for much more detail about building a healthy stockpile, but I would like to draw your attention to a few items that have a particularly long shelf life—and this could be a huge asset if we find ourselves facing a nuclear winter (Lembo 2019):

- **Honey:** This will last well past its expiration date because the sugar and lack of moisture make it difficult for bacteria to cause problems. You will start to see crystals forming in honey that's been kept for a long time, but it's still edible, and you can return the honey to its original state by heating it. Honey is rich in antioxidants, and it's a far healthier choice as a sweetener than other sugars—and, as an added bonus, it can help to heal wounds, so it's a good backup to have on hand (Shoemaker 2024).

- **Dry Rice:** This will last up to 30 years if it's kept in an oxygen-free environment. It provides a lot of beneficial vitamins and minerals, it's a good source of dietary fiber, and it's great for boosting your energy levels (Arnarson 2023).
- **Peanut Butter:** This lasts a surprisingly long time—between three and five years. It's because of the levels of Vitamin E and fat it contains, which delay oxidation and preserve it for longer. It's a good source of protein, and it's high in vitamins, minerals, and healthy fats—just be careful to choose a natural variety rather than a heavily processed version with a lot of added ingredients (Gunnars and Ajmera 2024).
- **Dried Beans and Lentils:** If they're stored correctly, these can last indefinitely. Canned beans will last for several years, too, but if you want supplies you can use many years down the line, it would be a good idea to stock dried ones as well. Beans are a good source of protein, antioxidants, and essential vitamins and minerals, and they're very good for your gut health (Villines 2023).
- **Powdered Milk:** Although this often has a "best before" date of little more than a year, the USDA says that it will last much longer than this, with some people

claiming a shelf-life of over 25 years. Another good source of protein is milk, which contains a range of vitamins and minerals, and it loses none of these in its powdered form (Kubala 2023).

PHYSICAL FITNESS

Just as your nutrition now will benefit you later, your physical fitness is something you want to have in good shape well in advance of a disaster. Each of these areas is something to work on if you want to make sure you're physically prepared for any survival situation, nuclear or otherwise (Carter 2023):

- **Sprinting:** It's true that you're not going to be doing any sprinting while you're sheltering, but you may need to quickly get medical help or move between locations after the fallout is over. You want to be able to move quickly. To hone this skill, try interval training, sprint drills, and short, high-intensity running bursts.
- **Agility:** You want to be able to change direction quickly, particularly if you're not already inside at the time of the blast. When you're working on your sprinting, try to include multi-directional drills to work on this skill. Lateral movements, cone drills, and directional changes will also help with this.
- **Strength:** When you evacuate, you're going to need to carry things—and there may come a time when you need to carry a person, too. You're going to need your strength. Use heavy weights and incorporate squats,

pull-ups, deadlifts, and overhead presses into your workout routine.
- **Cardio Fitness:** You won't be going anywhere immediately, but eventually, you may need to cover significant distances, possibly carrying a lot. A good level of cardio fitness will make this possible. To build this, I'd recommend running, jogging, and walking regularly, hiking over long distances, and rucking.
- **Flexibility:** Once it's possible to move around outside, you may be navigating a lot of destruction, which might require you to move through small spaces. You want to be able to do this as comfortably and efficiently as possible so that you don't find yourself trapped. To work on this skill, try stretching routines, yoga, and mobility exercises.

Some gyms run fitness programs designed to emulate those used by the Marines and the Navy Seals, and you can get versions you can do at home, too. This might be a good option for covering all of your bases when it comes to getting your fitness survival-ready.

All of this becomes a little more complicated when you have to shelter all day and have a limited supply of food. You may go into a crisis in good physical shape, but you also want to be able to maintain that fitness without expending too much energy (and therefore burning through more calories).

To keep your strength and fitness up during the disaster, try walking in place to keep up your cardio fitness, yoga to work on your strength, balance, and flexibility, and bodyweight exercises to build your endurance and strength. You also need to conserve your energy, though, so be careful not to overdo it (The Verdict Restaurant 2024). When your body is in crisis mode, you'll likely produce a lot of adrenaline, and your heart rate may often be elevated. This will already require more energy than you're used to using in a stationary position (Gordon 2023). This also means that if you can stay calm, you're going to conserve your energy. If you feel yourself panicking, focus on your breathing, try to return to a state of calm, and if you have to move between locations, do so slowly and carefully (unless there's a real need for you to hurry, of course).

MENTAL RESILIENCE

Your mental resilience is just as important as your physical fitness. It's this that will help you bounce back from setbacks, maintain the positive attitude your family needs, and make sensible decisions for your safety. Here's what it encompasses (Macwelch 2020):

- **Tenacity:** This is really about mental endurance and your ability to push yourself through even when things are hard. In a survival situation of any kind, your mental health is vulnerable, and this can make it difficult to channel your tenaciousness. To help with this, if you notice that you're feeling anxious, depressed, angry, or prone to irrational behavior, do what you can to remedy it through deep breathing, exercising if you can, and talking it through with your family.

- **Adaptability:** You need to be able to adapt as situations change, and this means you're going to need to be flexible and open to trying different approaches, which may mean abandoning a plan you'd been dead set on. Stubbornness can get in the way here, and it's easy to mistake it for tenacity, so you need to be aware of when it's at play. If something isn't working and you keep at it anyway rather than approaching the problem from a different angle, it's quite likely that it's stubbornness getting in your way, and you'll need to pay attention so that it doesn't hold you back.
- **Work Ethic:** Any emergency situation requires hard work, and you'll need to be able to persevere with a task until it's complete, trying new approaches as necessary. To build up your work ethic well in advance of a disaster, force yourself to do tasks you're naturally inclined to put off and avoid taking shortcuts.
- **Creativity:** There are few survival situations in which you won't have to come up with creative solutions, but sometimes, the fear of failure can hold us back and prevent our creativity from coming to the forefront. Remember that failure is helpful: It informs your next move. Don't be afraid to try an off-the-wall approach just because you're worried it might not work.
- **Positivity:** A positive mental attitude is a huge asset in an emergency, especially if you have a family whose morale you need to keep up. It isn't always easy to stay positive when you're in a dangerous or scary situation, but if you allow yourself to fall prey to pessimism, it could prevent you from taking the actions needed to

keep yourself and your family safe. Gratitude can be helpful for maintaining a positive attitude. If I find myself feeling pessimistic, I try to focus on the things I'm grateful for—no matter how small.

- **Acceptance:** You don't have to like what's going on, but you do need to be able to accept it. This is the reality you're dealing with, and if you deny it, you're liable to act misguidedly instead of being led by what's really happening.
- **Humor:** When you're able to laugh at the situation, you gain more power over it—there's a reason that gallows humor is so common in terrible situations. Being able to find the ironic or the comically absurd in a situation will have a therapeutic effect and work to relieve some of your anxiety.
- **Bravey:** Some people confuse this with an absence of fear, but in fact, fear is what makes a person brave. Bravery is about overcoming that fear, and this can be difficult when you're panicking. The secret here is to slow down, acknowledge your fear, and accept it. Once you're able to own it and prevent it from controlling you, you'll be able to use it as a tool for strength.
- **Motivation:** If you start to feel hopeless, you're in danger. If you lose hope, your urge to keep pushing forward will begin to wane. If you start to feel a lack of motivation, search for the things you want to survive for. Protecting your family is probably going to be a big one.

PROTECTING MENTAL HEALTH

In the event of a nuclear disaster, most people are going to go into survival mode. We're experiencing trauma, and this is likely to trigger the brain to resort to its trauma responses, fight, flight, or freeze, which limits our capacity to do anything more than the essentials. If you notice yourself or anyone in your family neglecting to take care of their basic needs, feeling unusually tired, struggling to regulate their emotions, lacking in focus, acting impulsively, or having difficulties with memory, they're probably in survival mode. It's important to acknowledge this and take steps to intervene so that it doesn't stand in the way of your ability to tackle the challenges that may come up along the way (Jefferson Center n.d., Young 2020).

If you notice signs of survival mode in yourself, treat yourself with compassion and acknowledge that your response is a natural one. If you're able to exercise, this may help you to shake off some energy and bring yourself into balance. Breathing exercises will help you again here, too, as will taking a moment to ground yourself in the present moment by tuning into your surroundings. Take it back to basics and focus on getting a decent amount of sleep and eating well (Young 2020).

Here are some strategies for protecting your mental health and warding off a descent into survival mode (Jefferson Center n.d.):

- **Practice self-compassion.** Acknowledge that the moment is difficult and that you're doing your best to cope with it. Allow yourself to make mistakes, remind

yourself that human beings aren't perfect, and release yourself from the pressure of negative thoughts.
- **Focus on self-regulation.** When you're in survival mode, you're often more focused on the future and whether you're going to make it, and this can make you act impulsively. You can bring yourself back to the present by regulating, which will be much easier if you're already practicing self-compassion. To self-regulate, again, focus on your breathing and pay attention to your surroundings, naming the things you can see, hear, smell, and touch to bring yourself into the present moment.
- **Practice self-care.** You won't have all the options available to you that you do in your regular life, but this doesn't mean that you can't take care of yourself as best you can within the limitations. Focus on getting enough sleep, moving your body, keeping yourself as clean as you can, and feeding yourself as well as possible.

HYGIENE

Hygiene remains important no matter what's happening, and while a nuclear crisis might make your usual routines and practices impossible, maintaining them as best you can is important. Washing your hands regularly to prevent the spread of germs is vital, and you'll have to do so more often if there's any chance that you've come into contact with radioactive materials, but it's also important not to wash them unnecessarily. You want your skin to build up its natural antibacterial oils in order to fight off germs, and you want to allow your immune system to work naturally. Essential oils are helpful here: They promote a natural way of keeping clean. Cedarwood and clove are good options because they have antibacterial, antiviral, and antiseptic properties, but you'll need to dilute them so they don't burn. A natural soap would be a good addition to your survival kit, too —it will last longer than a hand sanitizer, and it will double up as shampoo or laundry soap if you need it to (Mink 2016).

When it comes to washing and bathing with water, be sure that you're using water that's safe. As we saw earlier, tap water is unlikely to contain enough nuclear particles to make it harmful (as long as you don't consume it), and it should be fine for bathing. If, further into the aftermath, you find yourself navigating a wilderness survival situation, be cautious about water sources that could be contaminated. Even if you're far enough away from ground zero for radioactive materials not to be an issue, lakes, rivers, and streams could be contaminated in other ways. Always keep any rashes or wounds covered when bathing so that they don't become infected. For brushing your teeth, I personally wouldn't take the chance with tap water. I think it's worth sacrificing a small amount of your water supply for this job (CDC 2024).

THE REALITY OF A NUCLEAR WINTER

In the event of a full nuclear winter, survival may be all we can hope for, and normalcy may not return for many years, if it does at all. There are a few places, however, where researchers think survival may be easier under these circumstances. These are New Zealand, Australia, the Solomon Islands, Vanuatu, and

Iceland—countries believed to be the most likely to be able to continue producing food in the new climate. It's thought that only the most resilient countries will survive a nuclear winter, and these may be the best places to be if you're to be among the survivors (Sky News 2023).

The problem with this is that if a nuclear event significant enough to result in a nuclear winter were to happen, the chances of you being able to get to any of these countries are very slim. This is something you'd want to do now. My wife and I have discussed moving to Australia before, but this makes sense for us because we have family there. We don't plan on moving right now. We have a life where we are, and we want to make sure that we balance being prepared with living the life we have now fully.

TAKE ACTION!

Improving your health and fitness as an act of preparation is all very well, but it's helpful to know what areas you need to work on the most. Try these fitness tests to help you figure it out (Keeble 2024 and Quinn 2024):

- **Stability, Core Strength, and Upper Body Strength Test:** With your forearms on the ground, adopt a plank position and hold it for as long as possible without letting your form slip. The longer you can hold it, the better your core strength. If you want to test this further, try adding different positions as you hold the plank. Can you hold your right arm out for 15 seconds? How about your left leg? How about both at the same time? If you can do this, your core strength is very good; if not, you could benefit from more work here.

- **Sit-to-Stand Test:** To test your lower body strength, track the amount of time it takes you to stand from a seated position (with your arms crossed over your chest) and sit back down ten times. Men between the ages of 30 and 55 should be able to do this in 13 seconds, while women of the same age should be able to do it in 15. If you're between 56 and 65, you should be able to do it in 16 seconds if you're a man and 18 seconds if you're a woman.
- **Endurance and Muscular Strength Test:** You can use either a standard pushup position or a modified one with your knees on the ground to do this. Track how many pushups you can do within a minute without breaking form. To indicate excellent endurance and muscular strength, men between the ages of 30 and 39 would need to do 30 pushups. For men in their 40s, this drops to 25 and 21 if you're in your 50s. For women, it's 27 if you're in your 30s, 24 if you're in your 40s, and 21 if you're in your 50s.
- **Aerobic Fitness Test:** Test yourself by jogging or running for 12 minutes (after warming up). Measure the distance you moved in this time. To indicate excellent cardio fitness, men in their 30s need to cover 2,700 meters. In your 40s, it's 2,500 meters, and if you're over 50, it's 2,400 meters. For women, if you're in your 30s, you'll need to cover 2,500 meters. In your

40s, it's 2,300 meters, and if you're over 50, it's 2,200 meters.

There's a certain amount you can do to protect yourself and your family, but you're part of a much larger community, and whether a localized disaster or a full-scale global catastrophe happens, we'll need to rebuild the world. In the next chapter, we'll explore what that might look like.

10

THE WORST-CASE SCENARIO—POST-INCIDENT RECOVERY

We can be as prepared as we like, but there's no way of knowing for certain what a post-nuclear world will look like. In this chapter, we're going to focus on a larger-scale event because local disasters would most likely result in communities being evacuated and supported, ultimately allowing them to move somewhere that still has infrastructure. But if, for example, there was a nuclear war, this might be much less likely. This is the world we're going to look at in this chapter.

REBUILDING

There's been plenty of research into what the physical results of a full-scale nuclear war might be, but shockingly little into how we might return to any state of normality. A nuclear winter, the collapse of technology, the difficulties with food production, and the devastating amount of sickness and death are all very real concerns, but they wouldn't happen in a vacuum. We would also face political, economic, and social consequences that have barely been touched upon in research. Indeed, government planning is greatly lacking in what might be done in the aftermath of a nuclear war (Thomson and Ingram 2024).

What little research has been done, at least readily available to the public, is not recent. In *The Medical Implications of Nuclear War*, Hal Cochrane and Dennis Mileti explore the political, economic, and social consequences of such an event, but this was in the late 1980s, and the world has changed significantly since then. Even in their introduction, they say that there had been little social science research in earlier literature. "Much of the work was performed in the mid-1960s to mid-1970s and is therefore dated," they said, and their own writing now also falls into the same category (Cochrane and Mileti 1986).

In all likelihood, we'll all have to pull together to create resilient communities by sharing our skills, knowledge, and resources. This will mean joining forces with other families and coming up with systems to ensure that decisions are made fairly. We will only have limited supplies to work with, but we can do our best to ensure that all practices are sustainable within our limitations—this way, we'll be working toward a hopeful future rather than simply surviving. Skill sharing and education will be important: Anyone who has skills can play a vital role in building a new world by teaching others how to develop them and put them to use.

We can assume that there would be widespread efforts toward rebuilding and recovering, and I'm sure there would be much evidence of compassion and creativity involved in this process. But it's also likely that there would be a darker, more chaotic side of the story, a fear-driven one that gives rise to anarchy and misinformation (Thomson and Ingram 2024). I believe governments should be planning for economic and social rebuilding now; without it, we're going to be left largely to our own devices, and we may find ourselves trying to survive without critical industries like pharmaceuticals, agriculture, and electronics—all in the absence of law and order.

SURVIVING AMID THE CHAOS

If we ever managed to rebuild the world, it would take time, and much loss would be suffered along the way. There's no doubt that we'd need the survival skills we discussed in Chapter 8, but let's now put them in the context of a post-nuclear world (Food Bunker 2022):

- **Situational Awareness:** This is what will underpin your ability to source food and water, as well as shelter if you need it. It's going to be cold and dark, and you're probably going to be navigating through a lot of destruction. You're going to need your situational awareness and your mapping skills to familiarize yourself with the area and work out what resources you can use.
- **Repair and Mechanics Skills:** You only have to watch a movie set in a post-apocalyptic world to guess that you might be facing scenes in which vehicles or parts of vehicles litter the streets. With some basic skills, you

may be able to find necessary parts and repair abandoned vehicles, not to mention power generators and farming equipment.

- **Language Skills:** You're likely to meet people from a range of different cultures as whole communities are dispersed and relocating, and if you're able to speak a few different languages, you might find it easier to make alliances. This may also be a skill you can barter with.
- **Navigation and Travel Skills:** Food and water could be scarce, and you may need to travel to find them; it's also possible that it becomes too dangerous to stay where you are. Either way, you're going to need the navigational skills we discussed earlier. It might also be worth learning additional skills like sailing—that way, you have the option to escape to a different land mass if you need to.
- **Skills in Food Sourcing, Producing, and Preparing:** You may not have all the options you have right now, but if you have skills in this area, it will help you to find and prepare what food there is—and if you're lucky enough to come across a bounty, you're going to want to be able to preserve it.
- **First Aid and Medical Skills:** Without access to healthcare, you're going to need to be able to take care of yourself and others, addressing wounds and infections as they arise. You may have a hard time finding the necessary medications, but if you have some basic pharmacology knowledge, you'll at least know

what to look for. Some knowledge of herbal medicine will also help here.

- **Tool-Making Skills:** Mass production will have become a thing of the past, and you're going to need tools. This means you want to be able to repair ones you find or make new ones, so joinery, welding, and metalwork skills will be an asset.
- **Social and Communication Skills:** Collaborating with other people will allow you to share skills and resources and possibly even build a community. For this, you're going to need to be confident about bartering and working with other people.
- **Skills in Securing a Shelter:** Law enforcement is unlikely to be operating efficiently, if at all, and with survivors desperate for resources, making sure your base is secure will be essential. This means choosing somewhere that you can defend easily and fortify it with whatever resources you can find. Self-defense skills are important here, too.
- **Skills in Staying Inconspicuous:** In the absence of law enforcement, you want to stay under the radar as much as possible. This is sometimes referred to as making yourself "gray." Essentially, it means to downplay your skills and do everything you can not to stand out. Wear dark-colored clothes if you can, move about discreetly, and be aware of your surroundings, keeping your resources hidden (Gold 2024). If you're worried about the safety of the female members of your party, you may want to take steps to help them appear more boyish—

short haircuts, for example, gender-neutral clothes, and possibly even sports bras or binders to make it less easy for them to be quickly identified as female.

TAKE ACTION!

Survival in a post-apocalyptic world is one of the worst emergencies we can think about preparing for, and, depending on the extent of it, survival could be very difficult. I'm acutely aware of this, so I want to make our last activity light, fun, and useful for helping you prepare your children. Here are two more games to play with your kids to make prepping fun, both of which have been tried and tested by my family:

1. **Lights Out:** This will help your children navigate in the dark, and if this is something that scares them, it will also help them become more familiar with it and, therefore, less frightened. When it's dark outside, turn the lights out and try to go through your ordinary routines as a family. They'll quickly see that this is difficult. Then, you can get the flashlights out and continue. See if you can do the whole evening this way, even reading stories and playing games before bedtime.
2. **No Power:** This will help your kids get used to the idea of functioning without technology and teach them to adapt when they need to. It's a lot like Lights Out, except you're going to take it a step further. See if your family can live for a whole day without electricity. You might need to cook dinner outside on the grill or a camping stove. Perhaps you'll need to build a fire in the

backyard to stay warm. Let your children try to come up with creative solutions to problems that arise along the way.

A nuclear disaster is a terrifying concept, and I made myself quite anxious by researching nuclear war. I had to remind myself that although prepping is important, it's also important to appreciate what we have and live in the present moment. This is the message I'd like to leave you with as we close this final chapter. We're trying to prepare for the worst possible situation, but it isn't upon us yet. Your life right now is in the current world with your family. Prepare, by all means, but don't lose track of the value of this time or the life you have now.

ONE LAST MISSION!

The more of us who are prepared to survive come what may, the better. If you see the opportunity to share your knowledge and skills with others, please do so, and in the meantime, take a moment to share this guidance with more people.

Simply by sharing your honest opinion of this book and a little about how it's helped you with your preparation plans, you'll show new readers exactly where they can find it so that they too can do what they can to protect their families.

Thank you so much for your support. Remember: Stay healthy; stay strong; stay prepared!

Scan the QR code to leave your review.

CONCLUSION

We started this book on a very somber note, and that's not where I want us to end it. A nuclear disaster of any kind is going to change the world as we know it, and it will be the toughest survival challenge we could ever face ... but there's a certain amount you can do to prepare for it, and I hope that you've collected a good stock of ideas throughout our journey together.

What I want to do now is end on a story of hope, so I leave you with the positive spirit of Kenta Sato, a farmer who was affected by the disaster at Fukushima. The region in which he lived was protected by a mountain range, which kept radioactive fallout from falling on his land, but still, he was exposed to radiation. He sheltered at home for a month with his family as they watched the radiation levels increase on their detector. They were told they were safe, and they weren't included in the evacuation zone, but he now believes that his family was exposed to radiation. His land, however, remained uncontaminated, but each year, he gets his rice and fruit tested for safety. His produce is declared safe every time, but his sales have plummeted since the disaster. Perhaps this doesn't sound so positive, but Sato lives to tell the tale, and he refuses to give up on his land or his work (Beser 2016).

Sato and his family went through a deeply traumatic experience that still affects them to this day, but they survived. There's every chance that we can, too. I encourage you to work through the *Take Action!* activities peppered throughout the book, identify the skills you still need to work on, and do what you can to perfect them. The more prepared you are, the better chance of survival you have.

Finally, I'd like to remind you that living in the now is just as important as preparing for the future. To me, prepping should be fun as well as practical—it's an opportunity to spend time with your family while also teaching them essential survival skills. This is how I approach it, and honestly, I think if I didn't, I'd be riddled with worry most days. I don't want to prepare for the future by not living in the present, and I urge you to take this time to savor all the good things in your life while preparing for (rather than worrying about) what may happen in the future. Preparation is vital, but it should never come at the expense of your life today.

Ted Riley

ANSWERS FOR CHAPTER 2 QUIZ

1. What was the main reason for the Chornobyl accident?
    - *Human error*
2. Which natural disaster led to the nuclear disaster at Fukushima?
    - *Tsunami*
3. What is nuclear fission?
    - *The process of an atomic nucleus being broken down into smaller nuclei*
4. What is the name of the treaty preventing nuclear weapons testing?
    - *The Comprehensive Nuclear-Test-Ban Treaty*
5. When was the most recent serious nuclear power plant disaster?
    - *Fukushima in 2011*

ALSO BY TED RILEY

Would your family survive in lockdown if society were to collapse? Learn how to prepare your home now.

We are used to a world in which our homes are supplied with fresh water, gas, and electricity.

We're used to having our waste removed and our sanitary needs met.

These are all things we've come to expect, but what would happen if they were taken away?

Flooding, hurricanes, and pandemics are affecting areas we once thought were safe from disaster--we shouldn't take anything for granted.

In *When Crisis Hits Suburbia: A Modern-Day Prepping Guide to Effectively Bug In and Protect Your Family Home in a Societal Collapse,* you'll learn exactly what you need to know to prepare your home for an emergency. You'll find:

- The **6 key priorities of survival** and how to make sure you have them covered

- A clear guide for knowing when it's time to stay in, and when it's time to evacuate
- Top prepper **survival secrets** so that you always stay one step ahead of the rest
- A toolbox of information that allows you to choose what works best for your family
- **Practical tips** for preparing your children for worst-case scenarios without frightening them
- How to make sure your water supply is 100% safe at all times
- Comprehensive checklists for everything you need to stock in your home
- **Essential administrative tasks** you should have sorted in advance before a disaster strikes

And much more.

The ideal home is not only the home that keeps you and your family safe in good times, but it's the home that **keeps you safe no matter what**.

Prepare your home for the worst-case scenario and protect your family no matter what.

Scan the QR code to order your copy now.

Do you know how to stay healthy in the face of an emergency? Prepare now to keep your immune system on your side, no matter what happens tomorrow.

The chances of being stuck in our homes for long periods of time are greater than ever, and when disaster strikes, it can be difficult to get hold of crucial supplies.

Preppers have been evangelizing about food preservation and stockpiling for years. It turns out **they were right**, and now it's time to learn their secrets.

In *The Prepper's Pantry: Nutritional Bulk Food Prepping to Maintain a Healthy Diet and a Strong Immune System to Survive Any Crisis*, you'll find a **comprehensive guide** to preparing for good health in the face of an emergency. You'll discover:

- The **#1 way to stay healthy**, no matter what disaster is thrown your way
- Solid nutritional foundations for good health and strong immunity
- The importance of immune health in the event of an emergency
- 4 crucial food preparation **techniques** you'll need to adopt in order to stock your pantry efficiently
- A fool-proof guide to shopping, preparing, and storing your stocks for safe-keeping

- What **cupboard essentials** you should get a hold of now, and how to prolong their shelf-life
- **Lost skills** previous generations had down to a fine art, yet how you can pick these up once again

And much more.

You won't just be preparing to survive: **you'll be preparing to thrive**.

Know exactly how to prepare for good health in the face of a crisis.

Scan the QR code to order your copy now.

You can stockpile all the rice you like... but do you know how you're going to cook it if you're without power for months on end?

If the power grid fails, it's not just your lights that go out. It's your water supply. It's your heating and cooling system. It's all your usual ways of cooking food or doing the laundry.

Without the grid, life as we know it changes in an instant.

Are you prepared for that?

In *Prepare Your Home for a Sudden Grid-Down Situation*, you'll discover:

- The most likely causes of a grid-down situation -- and how they'll affect your family
- **Easy immediate short-term solutions to see you through the first few days of disaster**
- Grid-down cooking options (you'll be amazed by how many ways there are to feed your family a delicious hot meal without your cooker)
- **A full range of emergency backup solutions you can fall back on if you're currently totally reliant on the grid**
- What to do when cash means nothing -- think outside the box to make sure your family thrives

- **The ultimate guide to making sure your family has access to clean, safe water (no matter what's going on outside)**
- Exactly what you can do to stay healthy and well when the toilet won't flush, the washing machine's useless, and a long hot bath is out of the question
- Everything you need to know about communicating with the outside world in a grid-down emergency
- **A clear breakdown of your off-grid power options -- so you can plan now for any unexpected event**
- Easy DIY projects you can work through right now to sharpen your skills and prepare for the worst

And much more.

If you thought your stash of canned beans and laundry supplies was enough to see you through an emergency, think again. It's a great start… but have you thought about how you're going to cook those beans? Do you know how you're going to wash your clothes?

Being prepared is about more than stocking up. It's about thinking outside the box and learning essential survival skills.

Scan the QR code to order your copy now.

No one likes to think of the worst-case scenario... But if you're unprepared, the 'worst case' could become much worse than you ever imagined...

We all hope we'll never need an emergency plan.

But the hard truth is that you need one to **keep yourself and your family safe in case the unthinkable happens.**

Most advice around bugging out in a disaster situation is focused purely on what's in that bag... and while it's crucial to get your kit right, it's only one piece of the puzzle.

The bug-out bag is important, but a bug-out bag without a complete plan behind it is useless.

In this **comprehensive guide** to bugging out, you'll find **everything you need to keep your family safe if you must evacuate your home** you'll discover:

- **How to recognize the signs that evacuation is your best option**
- The crucial acronym that will help you assess any situation
- How to choose the perfect bug-out location for your family (including the #1 mistake most people make when choosing their spot)

- **Your guide to building the ultimate bug-out bag**
- Essential skills and training tips to ensure the whole family is prepared for the worst
- **Everything you need to know about route planning and transportation in an emergency**
- The extra details you need to consider if you'll be **bugging out with your children, elderly relatives, or pets**
- How to make your evacuation route into a treasure trove of essential supplies
- All your safety and security questions answered
- **Practical activities to prepare your family and equip them with life-saving skills**

And much more.

If you're not convinced that your family needs a bug-out plan, all you need to do is look at the **rising number of natural disasters** creeping up across the world… Wouldn't you rather be prepared to handle anything?

Prepare your family to thrive and survive any worst-case scenario!

Scan the QR code to order your copy now.

If you haven't already, don't forget to access your free
Emergency Information Planner

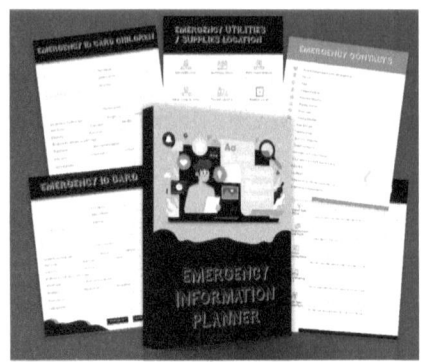

Follow the link below to receive your copy:
www.tedrileyauthor.com
Or by accessing the QR code:

You can also join our Facebook community **Suburban Prepping with Ted**, or contact me directly via ted@tedrileyauthor.com.

REFERENCES

Abrams, Herbert L. "Medical Supply and Demand in a Post-nuclear-War World" in Solomon, Fred, Robert Q. Marston, Lewis Thomas, and Steering Committee for the Symposium on the Medical Implications of Nuclear War. *The Medical Implications of Nuclear War*. Washington: National Academies Press, 1986.

"Accidents at Nuclear Power Plants and Cancer Risk." National Cancer Institute. Accessed January 31, 2025. https://www.cancer.gov/about-cancer/causes-prevention/risk/radiation/nuclear-accidents-fact-sheet.

Adamant, Ashley. October 15, 2018. "Can You Survive a Nuclear Winter?" Practical Self Reliance. Accessed January 31, 2025. https://practicalselfreliance.com/survive-nuclear-winter/.

Adamant, Ashley. February 25, 2018. "Choosing a Survival Seed Bank." Practical Self Reliance. Accessed January 31, 2025. https://practicalselfreliance.com/choosing-survival-seed-bank/.

Adamant, Ashley. August 19, 2021. "How to Freeze Dry Food at Home." Practical Self Reliance. Accessed January 31, 2025. https://practicalselfreliance.com/freeze-dry-food/.

"Advice for the Public on Protection in Case of a Nuclear Detonation." n.d. ICRP. Accessed January 31, 2025. https://www.icrp.org/page.asp?id=611.

"Backgrounder on Radioactive Waste." January 26, 2024. United States Nuclear Regulatory Commission. Accessed January 31, 2025. https://www.nrc.gov/reading-rm/doc-collections/fact-sheets/radwaste.html.

Barnes, Adam. June 3, 2023. "How to Build a Cheap DIY Underground Bunker to Protect You from Nuclear Fallout, in 6 Steps." Business Insider. Accessed January 31, 2025. https://www.businessinsider.com/cheap-diy-underground-bunker-fallout-shelter-2023-5.

Baumgart, Jake. July 15, 2024. "The Most Essential Things to Stock In Your Bomb Shelter." Ranker. Accessed January 31, 2025. https://www.ranker.com/list/bomb-shelter-essentials/jakebaumgart.

"Before, During, and After an Emergency." October 24, 2024. CDC. Accessed January 31, 2025. https://www.cdc.gov/disasters-and-children/before-during-after/index.html.

Bendix, Aria. n.d. "A Full-scale Nuclear Winter Would Trigger a Global Famine. A Disaster Expert Put Together a Doomsday Diet to Save Humanity." Business Insider. Last modified January 10, 2020. https://www.businessinsider.com/how-to-survive-after-nuclear-war-what-to-eat-2020-1.

Bendix, Aria, Morgan McFall-Johnsen, and Adam Barnes. July 21, 2023. January 10, 2020. "How to Survive Nuclear War After a Bomb is Dropped: What to Do, How to Prepare." Business Insider. Accessed January 31, 2025. https://www.businessinsider.com/guide-to-protect-yourself-nuclear-attack-before-after-bomb-2022-3.

Benoit, Matt. May 7, 2022. "Could Humans Grow Food During a Nuclear Winter?" Discover Magazine. Accessed January 31, 2025. https://www.discovermagazine.com/environment/could-humans-grow-food-during-a-nuclear-winter.

"Bomb Shelters and Underground Bunkers: The Importance to Remove CO2." n.d. Alfaintek. Accessed January 31, 2025. https://www.alfaintek.com/blog/underground-bunkers-bomb-shelters.html.

Bradley, Charlie. June 21, 2024. "Food Set to Be Grown Near Chornobyl 38 Years After Nuclear Disaster." Express.co.uk. Accessed January 31, 2025. https://www.express.co.uk/news/world/1913986/Chornobyl-food-grown-nuclear-disaster.

Brahambhatt, Rupendra. February 25, 2023. "Sheltering Miles from a Nuclear Blast May Not Be Enough to Survive Unless You Know Where to Hide, New Calculations Show." Business Insider. Accessed January 31, 2025. https://www.businessinsider.com/where-hide-during-nuclear-blast-room-corners-avoid-hallway-doors-2023-2.

"A Brief History of Nuclear Accidents Worldwide." October 1, 2013. Union of Concerned Scientists. Accessed January 31, 2025. https://www.ucsusa.org/Resources/Brief-History-Nuclear-Accidents-Worldwide.

Bromet, Evelyn J. "Emotional Consequences of Nuclear Power Plant Disasters." *Health Physics* 106, no. 2 (2014), 206-210. doi:10.1097/hp.0000000000000012.

Bromet, Evelyn J., and Johan M. Havenaar. November, 2007. "Psychological and Perceived Health Effects of the Chornobyl Disaster: A 20-Year Review." The Radiation Safety Journal Health Physics. Accessed January 31, 2025. https://journals.lww.com/health-physics/abstract/2007/11000/psychological_and_perceived_health_effects_of_the.17.aspx.

"Build A Kit." US Department of Homeland Security. Accessed January 31, 2025. https://www.ready.gov/kit.

Burch, Kelly. June 16, 2023. "Where to Find Food and Water That's Safe to Eat in the Event of a Nuclear Apocalypse." Business Insider. Accessed January 31, 2025. https://www.businessinsider.com/nuclear-apocalypse-safe-food-water.

Business Insider. December 19, 2022. "Here's What You Actually Need in a Nuclear Survival Kit." We Are The Mighty. Last modified March 31, 2018. https://www.wearethemighty.com/mighty-trending/heres-what-you-actually-need-in-a-nuclear-survival-kit/.

"Caring for Your Mental Health." December, 2024. National Institute of Mental Health (NIMH). Accessed January 31, 2025. https://www.nimh.nih.gov/health/topics/caring-for-your-mental-health.

"Chornobyl Accident 1986." n.d. World Nuclear Association. Accessed January 31, 2025. https://world-nuclear.org/information-library/safety-and-security/safety-of-plants/Chornobyl-accident.

Cochrane, Hal and Dennis Mileti. "The Consequences of Nuclear War: An Economic and Social Perspective" in Solomon, Fred, Robert Q. Marston, Lewis Thomas, and Steering Committee for the Symposium on the Medical Implications of Nuclear War. *The Medical Implications of Nuclear War*. Washington: National Academies Press, 1986.

Coleman, Beverly. January 23, 2024. "Food Preservation Methods and Guidance." Human Focus. Accessed January 31, 2025. https://humanfocus.co.uk/blog/food-preservation-methods-and-guidance/.

"Coping with Disaster." n.d. US Department of Homeland Security. Accessed January 31, 2025. https://www.ready.gov/coping-disaster.

Coughlin, Daniel. September 25, 2024. "Affordable Bunkers to Survive the Apocalypse." Love Property. Accessed January 31, 2025. https://www.loveproperty.com/gallerylist/78262/affordable-bunkers-to-survive-the-apocalypse.

"Crops Near Chornobyl Still Contaminated." December 17, 2020. ScienceDaily. Accessed January 31, 2025. https://www.sciencedaily.com/releases/2020/12/201217135254.htm.

de Dreuzy, Pierre, and Andrea Gilli. November 29, 2022. "Russia's Nuclear Coercion in Ukraine." Nato Review. https://www.nato.int/docu/review/articles/2022/11/29/russias-nuclear-coercion-in-ukraine/index.html.

"Dealing with Nuclear War Anxiety." January 31, 2023. ICAN. Accessed January 31, 2025. https://www.icanw.org/dealing_with_nuclear_anxiety.

DeNardi, Candice. n.d. "Fact Sheet: The Basics of Nuclear Weapons." Center for Arms Control and Non-Proliferation. Accessed January 31, 2025. https://armscontrolcenter.org/fact-sheet-the-basics-of-nuclear-weapons/.

"Detecting Radiation." n.d. United States Nuclear Regulatory Committee. Accessed January 31, 2025. https://www.nrc.gov/about-nrc/radiation/health-effects/detection-radiation.html.

"Domestic Nuclear Shelters." 1981. Central Office of Information. Accessed January 31, 2025. https://www.atomica.co.uk/shelters/main.htm.

"Economic Impacts of a Nuclear Weapon Detonation." March, 2015. Article36. Accessed January 31, 2025. https://article36.org/wp-content/uploads/2015/08/Economic-impact.pdf.

"8 Things You Need When Setting Up a Survival Bunker." n.d. Leatherman. Accessed January 31, 2025. https://www.leatherman.com/blog/items-you-need-when-setting-up-a-survival-bunker.html.

"Electromagnetic Pulse (EMP) Following a Nuclear Detonation - Radiation Emergency Medical Management." January 2, 2025. Radiation Emergency Medical Management. Accessed January 31, 2025. https://remm.hhs.gov/EMP.htm.

"11 Off-Grid Communication Methods: Staying Connected in Emergencies and Remote Areas," September 18, 2023. Survival Frog. Accessed January 31, 2025. https://www.survivalfrog.com/blogs/survival/11-off-grid-communication-methods-staying-connected-in-emergencies-and-remote-areas.

"Emerging Technologies and Nuclear Risks." n.d. ICAN. Accessed January 31, 2025. https://www.icanw.org/emergingtechnologies.

Emerging Technology from the arXiv. April 17, 2015. "The Chances of Another Chornobyl Before 2050? 50%, Say Safety Specialists." MIT Technology Review. Accessed January 31, 2025. https://www.technologyreview.com/2015/04/17/168600/the-chances-of-another-Chornobyl-before-2050-50-say-safety-specialists/.

"Empower Yourself: Essential Self-Defence Strategies for Preppers." October 24, 2024. Hugginsattic. Accessed January 31, 2025. https://hugginsattic.co.uk/blogs/prepping/empower-yourself-essential-self-defence-strategies-for-preppers.

"Evacuation." n.d. US Department of Homeland Security. Accessed January 31, 2025. https://www.ready.gov/evacuation.

"Family Disaster Plan." n.d. The Disaster Center. Accessed January 31, 2025. https://disastercenter.com/New%20Guide/Family%20Disaster%20Plan.html

"5 Useful Skills to Have in an Apocalypse." n.d. Bushcraft Buddy. Accessed January 31, 2025. https://bushcraftbuddy.com/5-useful-skills-to-have-in-an-apocalypse/.

Fohrman, Ian. October 30, 2020. "The Beginner's Guide to Hunting." Outside Online. Accessed January 31, 2025. https://www.outsideonline.com/outdoor-adventure/exploration-survival/beginners-guide-to-hunting/.

"Food, Drinking Water, and Medicine Safety in a Radiation Emergency." April 15, 2024. CDC. Accessed January 31, 2025. https://www.cdc.gov/radiation-emergencies/safety/food-drinking-water-medicine-safety.html.

"Food, Drinking Water, and Medicine Safety in a Radiation Emergency." n.d. CDC. Accessed January 31, 2025. https://www.cdc.gov/radiation-emergencies/safety/food-drinking-water-medicine-safety.html.

"4 Ways Parents Can Protect Their Mental Well-being During a Crisis." July 11, 2023. UNICEF South Asia. n.d. https://www.unicef.org/rosa/stories/4-ways-parents-can-protect-their-mental-well-being-during-crisis.

"Frequently Asked Questions About Potassium Iodide." August 23, 2024. United States Nuclear Regulatory Committee. Accessed January 31, 2025. https://www.nrc.gov/about-nrc/emerg-preparedness/about-emerg-preparedness/potassium-iodide/ki-faq.html.

"Fukushima Disaster: What Happened at the Nuclear Plant?" August 23, 2023. BBC News. Accessed January 31, 2025. https://www.bbc.co.uk/news/world-asia-56252695.

Furneaux, Ky. December 11, 2024. "How to Survive a Nuclear Attack." WikiHow. Accessed January 31, 2025. https://www.wikihow.com/Survive-a-Nuclear-Attack.

"Geiger-Mueller Counter." March 9, 2021. United States Nuclear Regulatory Committee. Accessed January 31, 2025. https://www.nrc.gov/reading-rm/basic-ref/glossary/geiger-mueller-counter.html.

Gold, Sean. September 26, 2024. "Best Lantern for Prepping and Survival." TruePrepper. Accessed January 31, 2025. https://trueprepper.com/best-survival-lantern/.

Gold, Sean. August 12, 2024. "How to Be a Gray Man." TruePrepper. Accessed January 31, 2025. https://trueprepper.com/gray-man/.

Goldbach, Josh, and Mason Martinez. February 14, 2024. "How to Make Fire

Without Matches or a Lighter: 9 Easy Ways." WikiHow. Accessed January 31, 2025. https://www.wikihow.com/Make-Fire-Without-Matches-or-a-Lighter.

Goldmann, Emily, and Sandro Galea. "Mental health consequences of disasters." *Annu Rev Public Health*, October 2013, 169-83.

Gonçalves, Paula. June 4, 2022. "Nuclear Disaster: What Food is Needed to Ensure Survival?" Meteored. Accessed January 31, 2025. https://www.yourweather.co.uk/news/science/nuclear-disaster-food-survival-agriculture-radiation.html.

Gordon, Yvonne. February 22, 2023. "Survival Situation? Staying Calm and Conserving Energy is Key." Outdoors with Bear Grylls. Accessed January 31, 2025. https://outdoors.com/how-bear-grylls-conserves-energy-in-survival-situations/.

"A Guide to Common Medicinal Herbs." n.d. University of Rochester Medical Center. Accessed January 31, 2025. https://www.urmc.rochester.edu/encyclopedia/content?contenttypeid=1&contentid=1169.

Harigane, Mayumi, Yoshitake Takebayashi, Michio Murakami, Masaharu Maeda, Rie Mizuki, Yuichi Oikawa, Saori Goto, et al. "Higher psychological distress experienced by evacuees relocating outside Fukushima after the nuclear accident: The Fukushima Health Management Survey." *International Journal of Disaster Risk Reduction* 52 (January 2021), 101962. doi:10.1016/j.ijdrr.2020.101962.

Haynes, Gavin. March 11, 2019. "DIY Doomsday Food Kits: How to Eat Well After the Apocalypse." The Guardian. Last modified March 11, 2018. https://www.theguardian.com/lifeandstyle/shortcuts/2018/mar/11/diy-doomsday-food-kits-how-to-eat-well-after-the-apocalypse.

"Healthy Diet." n.d. World Health Organization (WHO). Accessed January 31, 2025. https://www.who.int/initiatives/behealthy/healthy-diet.

Henry, Pat. January 10, 2014. "How to Get Your Family on Board With Prepping." The Prepper Journal. Accessed January 31, 2025. https://thepreperjournal.com/2014/01/10/get-family-on-board-with-prepping/.

Hori, A. January 20, 2021. "Coming to Terms with Fukushima Disaster-related Trauma and Earlier Trauma by Constructing a New Identity. About a Case." Radioprotection. Accessed January 31, 2025. https://www.radioprotection.org/articles/radiopro/full_html/2020/06/radiopro200078/radiopro200078.html.

"How Do Nuclear Weapons Work?" September 29, 2016. Union of Concerned

Scientists. Accessed January 31, 2025. https://www.ucsusa.org/resources/how-nuclear-weapons-work.

"How Many Nuclear Power Plants Are in the United States, and Where are They Located?" n.d. US Energy Information Administration (EIA). Accessed January 31, 2025. https://www.eia.gov/tools/faqs/faq.php?id=207&t=3.

"How to Protect Electronics Against an EMP (Electromagnetic Pulse)." June 19, 2023. Underwater Kinetics. Accessed January 31, 2025. https://uwk.com/blogs/blog/how-to-protect-electronics-against-an-emp-electromagnetic-pulse.

"How to Raise a Family of Survival Preppers." January 4, 2022. Famous Ashley Grant. Accessed January 31, 2025. https://famousashleygrant.com/how-to-raise-a-family-of-survival-preppers/.

"How to Talk to Children about Difficult Topics." n.d. NSPCC. Accessed January 31, 2025. https://www.nspcc.org.uk/keeping-children-safe/support-for-parents/talking-about-difficult-topics/.

"Hunter Education." n.d. US Fish and Wildlife Services. Accessed January 31, 2025. https://www.fws.gov/program/hunter-education.

"Immediate Action: Shelter, Then Evacuate." n.d. Monmouth County, N.J. Accessed January 31, 2025. https://www.co.monmouth.nj.us/documents/118/IMMEDIATE_ACTION_SHELTER_THEN_EVACUATE.pdf.

"The Impact of a Nuclear War." Campaign for Nuclear Disarmament. Last modified March 22, 2023. https://cnduk.org/resources/the-impact-of-a-nuclear-war/.

Italie, Leanne. March 16, 2022. "Talking to Kids About Nuclear Tensions? Experts Advise Telling the Truth." PBS News. Accessed January 31, 2025. https://www.pbs.org/newshour/education/talking-to-kids-about-nuclear-tensions-experts-advise-telling-the-truth.

Ito, Naomi, Nobuaki Moriyama, Ayako Furuyama, Hiroaki Saito, Toyoaki Sawano, Isamu Amir, Mika Sato, et al. "Why Do They Not Come Home? Three Cases of Fukushima Nuclear Accident Evacuees." *International Journal of Environmental Research and Public Health* 20, no. 5 (February 2023), 4027. doi:10.3390/ijerph20054027.

Jehn, Florian U., Farrah J. Dingal, Aron Mill, Ekaterina Ilin, Cheryl Harrison, Michael Y. Roleda, and David Denkenberger. "Seaweed as a resilient food solution in nuclear winter." *Advancing Earth and Space Sciences* 12, no. 1 (January 2024). doi:10.5194/egusphere-egu23-1871.

Jones, Edgar. May 16, 2023. "Overlooked Trauma of Nuclear Bomb Survivors."

BPS. Accessed January 31, 2025. https://www.bps.org.uk/psychologist/overlooked-trauma-nuclear-bomb-survivors.

Jones, Kylene. n.d. "A Wise Prepper's Guide to Bartering Skills and Supplies." The Provident Prepper. Accessed January 31, 2025. https://theprovidentprepper.org/a-wise-preppers-guide-to-bartering-skills-and-supplies/.

Jones, Kylene. n.d. "Raising Confident Self-Reliant Kid Preppers: 14 Essential Skills." The Provident Prepper. Accessed January 31, 2025. https://theprovidentprepper.org/raising-confident-self-reliant-kid-preppers-14-essential-skills/.

Kearny, Cresson. 2004. "Nuclear War Survival Skills." Oregon Institute of Science and Medicine. Accessed January 31, 2025. https://www.oism.org/nwss/s73p917.htm.

Kemp, Rob. November 12, 2020. "The Future of Farming Is Inside This Bomb Shelter." Popular Mechanics. Accessed January 31, 2025. https://www.popularmechanics.com/science/a34618094/future-farming-underground/.

Kim, Alex. 2015. "What Is Happening for the Fukushima Evacuees? : The Dislocated People of the Fukushima Disaster." Disaster Archipelago: Japan. Accessed January 31, 2025. https://commons.trincoll.edu/disasterarchipelago/?page_id=1011.

Kristensen, Hans, Matt Korda, Eliana Johns, Mackenzie Knight, and Kate Kohn. March 29, 2024. "Status of World Nuclear Forces." Federation of American Scientists. Accessed January 31, 2025. https://fas.org/initiative/status-world-nuclear-forces/.

Kubala, Jillian. March 15, 2023. "Are Ginger Shots Healthy? Benefits, Downsides, and Recipe." Healthline. Accessed January 31, 2025. https://www.healthline.com/nutrition/ginger-shots.

Lembo, Allie. July 2, 2019. "14 Foods to Keep in Your Bunker to Survive the Apocalypse." Business Insider. Accessed January 31, 2025. https://www.businessinsider.com/long-lasting-foods-apocalypse-2018-10.

Lynch, Bryan. July 7, 2022. "How to Prepare Your Family for a Survival Situation." PREPARED4X. Accessed January 31, 2025. https://prepared4x.com/en-gb/blogs/news/how-to-prepare-your-family-for-a-survival-situation.

MacWelch, Tim. October 4, 2019. "Survival Skills: 10 Ways to Purify Water." Outdoor Life. Accessed January 31, 2025. https://www.outdoorlife.com/survival-skills-ways-to-purify-water/.

Macwelch, Tim. September 12, 2019. "Survival Sanitation: Dealing with the "S" in SHTF." RECOIL OFFGRID. Accessed January 31, 2025. https://www. offgridweb.com/survival/survival-sanitation-dealing-with-the-s-in-shtf/.

Maeda, Masaharu, Misari Oe, and Yuriko Suzuki. "Psychosocial effects of the Fukushima disaster and current tasks: Differences between natural and nuclear disasters." *J. Natl. Inst. Public Health* 67, no. 1 (2018), 50-58.

"Major Nuclear Reactor Incidents." n.d. Atomicarchive.com: Exploring the History, Science, and Consequences of the Atomic Bomb. Accessed January 31, 2025. https://www.atomicarchive.com/almanac/accidents/accidents.html.

"Mapped: The World's Nuclear Power Plants." March 8, 2016. Carbon Brief. Accessed January 31, 2025. https://www.carbonbrief.org/mapped-the-worlds-nuclear-power-plants/.

McCarthy, Claire, and Scott Needle. "Disasters and Your Family: Be Prepared." HealthyChildren.org. Accessed January 31, 2025. https://www.healthychildren.org/English/safety-prevention/at-home/Pages/Getting-Your-Family-Disaster-Ready.aspx.

McDonagh, Shannon. April 7, 2021. "The Underground Vegetable Farm Thriving in London's Wartime Bunkers." Euronews. Accessed January 31, 2025. https://www.euronews.com/green/2021/04/07/the-underground-vegetable-farm-thriving-in-wartime-bunkers-below-london.

Mecklin, John. January 28, 2025. "2025 Doomsday Clock Statement." Bulletin of the Atomic Scientists. Accessed January 31, 2025. https://thebulletin.org/doomsday-clock/2025-statement/nuclear-risk/.

Melley, Brendan G. 2017. "Nuclear Terrorism – Imminent Threat?" Center for the Study of Weapons of Mass Destruction. Accessed January 31, 2025. https://wmdcenter.ndu.edu/Portals/97/Documents/Publications/Articles/Nuclear_Terrorism_Imminent_Threat.pdf?ver=2017-11-17-103912-223.

Mello-Klein, Cody. April 11, 2024. "What is 'Fallout'? Physicist Breaks Down the Science of Amazon's Sci-fi Show and the Horrifying Reality of Nuclear Radiation." Northeastern Global News. Accessed January 31, 2025. https://news.northeastern.edu/2024/04/11/fallout-nuclear-radiation/.

Mertins, Brian. n.d. "12 Easy Ways to Navigate Without A Compass." Nature Mentoring. Accessed January 31, 2025. https://nature-mentor.com/navigate-without-compass/.

Muehling, Eldon. March 16, 2011. "The Dangers of Nuclear Radiation in Water." My Pure Water. Accessed January 31, 2025. https://mypurewater.com/blog/2011/03/16/the-dangers-of-nuclear-radiation-in-water/.

Mulhollem, Jeff. March 29, 2022. "How Would a Nuclear Winter Impact Food Production?" The Pennsylvania State University. Accessed January 31, 2025. https://www.psu.edu/news/research/story/how-would-nuclear-winter-impact-food-production.

Newkey-Burden, Chas. October 29, 2024. "Where is the Safest Place in a Nuclear Attack?" The Week. Last modified October 29, 2024. https://theweek.com/nuclear-weapons/958055/the-safest-place-to-be-in-a-nuclear-attack.

Newman, Tim. July 13, 2023. "X-rays: Overview, Side Effects, Risks, and More." Medical and Health Information. Accessed January 31, 2025. https://www.medicalnewstoday.com/articles/219970.

"News and Terrorism, Communicating in a Crisis." n.d. US Department of Homeland Security. Accessed January 31, 2025. https://www.dhs.gov/xlibrary/assets/prep_nuclear_fact_sheet.pdf.

"NOAA Weather Radio." n.d. National Weather Service. Accessed January 31, 2025. https://www.weather.gov/nwr/.

"Nuclear Blasts: Frequently Asked Questions." April 10, 2024. CDC. Accessed January 31, 2025. https://www.cdc.gov/radiation-emergencies/about/nuclear-blast-faq.html.

"Nuclear Bunkers and Fallout Shelters." n.d. Subterranean Spaces. Accessed January 31, 2025. https://www.subterraneanspaces.co.uk/nuclear-bunker-fallout-shelter.

"Nuclear Detonation Preparedness: Communicating in the Immediate Aftermath." April, 2024. US Department of Homeland Security. Accessed January 31, 2025. https://www.fema.gov/sites/default/files/documents/fema_nuclear-detonation-preparedness_communicating-in-the-immediate-aftermath_v3_2024.pdf.

"Nuclear Explosion and Radiation Emergencies." n.d. American Red Cross. Accessed January 31, 2025. https://www.redcross.org/get-help/how-to-prepare-for-emergencies/types-of-emergencies/nuclear-explosion-radiation-emergencies.html.

"Nuclear Fallout Safety: Protecting Yourself and Your Loved Ones." June 23, 2023. RT Technologies. Accessed January 31, 2025. https://www.rtlasersafety.com/post/nuclear-fallout-safety-protecting-yourself-and-your-loved-ones.

"Nuclear Power 101." January 5, 2022. NRDC. Accessed January 31, 2025. https://www.nrdc.org/stories/nuclear-power-101.

"Nuclear Power and the Environment." US Energy Information Administration (EIA). Last modified November 7, 2022. https://www.eia.gov/energyexplained/nuclear/nuclear-power-and-the-environment.php.

"Nuclear Power in the World Today." January 6, 2025. World Nuclear Association. Accessed January 31, 2025. https://world-nuclear.org/information-library/current-and-future-generation/nuclear-power-in-the-world-today.

"Nuclear." n.d. Ready NC. Accessed January 31, 2025. https://www.readync.gov/stay-informed/north-carolina-hazards/nuclear.

"Nuclear." n.d. UNODA – United Nations Office for Disarmament Affairs. Accessed January 31, 2025. https://disarmament.unoda.org/nuclear/.

"Oklahoma." n.d. United States Nuclear Regulatory Commission. Accessed January 31, 2025. https://www.nrc.gov/info-finder/region-state/oklahoma.html.

"Planning for the Worst: Emergency Food Storage for Preppers." June 11, 2022. Food Bunker. Accessed January 31, 2025. https://foodbunker.co.uk/blogs/prepping/planning-for-the-worst-emergency-food-storage-for-preppers.

"Post Apocalyptic Survival Guide: Navigating the Doomsday Call Fallout." June 18, 2024. Faster Capital. Accessed January 31, 2025. https://fastercapital.com/content/Post-Apocalyptic-Survival-Guide--Navigating-the-Doomsday-Call-Fallout.html.

"Potassium Iodide (KI)." January 30, 2025. CDC. Accessed January 31, 2025. https://www.cdc.gov/radiation-emergencies/treatment/potassium-iodide.html.

"Pretend Games to Help Children Develop Preparedness Skills." n.d. Mom Prepared. Accessed January 31, 2025. https://momwithaprep.com/10-great-pretend-games-to-help-your-children-develop-preparedness-skills/.

"Prospect of Nuclear Accident 'Dangerously Close' at Zaporizhzhia Power Plant in Ukraine, International Atomic Energy Agency Chief Warns Security Council." United Nations. April 15, 2024. Accessed January 31, 2025. https://press.un.org/en/2024/sc15662.doc.htm.

"Protect and Survive." 1976. Central Office of Information. Accessed January 31, 2025. https://www.roc-heritage.co.uk/uploads/7/6/8/9/7689271/protectandsurvive.pdf.

"Rad Resilient City Initiative." n.d. Johns Hopkins Center for Health Security. Accessed January 31, 2025. https://centerforhealthsecurity.org/our-work/research-projects/project-archive/rad-resilient-city-initiative.

"Radiation and Health Effects." April 29, 2024. World Nuclear Association. Accessed January 31, 2025. https://world-nuclear.org/information-library/safety-and-security/radiation-and-health/radiation-and-health-effects.

"Radiation and Health." July 7, 2023. World Health Organization (WHO). Accessed January 31, 2025. https://www.who.int/news-room/questions-and-answers/item/radiation-and-health.

"Radiation Emergencies." n.d. US Department of Homeland Security. Accessed January 31, 2025. https://www.ready.gov/radiation.

"Radiation Injuries." n.d. Global First Aid Reference Centre. Accessed January 31, 2025. https://www.globalfirstaidcentre.org/radiation-injuries/.

"Radiation Sickness." June 11, 2024. Cleveland Clinic. Accessed January 31, 2025. https://my.clevelandclinic.org/health/diseases/24328-radiation-sickness.

"Radiation Sickness." February 13, 2024. Mayo Clinic. Accessed January 31, 2025. https://www.mayoclinic.org/diseases-conditions/radiation-sickness/symptoms-causes/syc-20377058.

"Radiation Sickness." July 1, 2023. MedlinePlus. Accessed January 31, 2025. https://medlineplus.gov/ency/article/000026.htm.

"Radiation Sickness." n.d. Mount Sinai. Accessed January 31, 2025. https://www.mountsinai.org/health-library/injury/radiation-sickness.

"Radioactive Fallout From Nuclear Weapons Testing." n.d. United States Environmental Protection Agency. Accessed January 31, 2025. https://www.epa.gov/radtown/radioactive-fallout-nuclear-weapons-testing.

"Radioactive Fallout." n.d. atomicarchive.com. Accessed January 31, 2025. https://www.atomicarchive.com/science/effects/radioactive-fallout.html.

"Radioactive Waste." n.d. Simpsons Wiki. Accessed January 31, 2025. https://simpsons.fandom.com/wiki/Radioactive_waste.

"Radioactivity in Food After a Nuclear Emergency." July 7, 2023. World Health Organization (WHO). Accessed January 31, 2025. https://www.who.int/news-room/questions-and-answers/item/radioactivity-in-food-after-a-nuclear-emergency.

Rao, Rahul. January 20, 2023. "The Best—and Worst—Places to Shelter After a Nuclear Blast." Popular Science. Accessed January 31, 2025. https://www.popsci.com/science/how-to-survive-a-nuclear-bomb-shockwave/.

Rasmussen, Joel, and Petter B. Wikström. "Returning Home after Decontamination? Applying the Protective Action Decision Model to a

Nuclear Accident Scenario." *International Journal of Environmental Research and Public Health* 19, no. 12 (June 2022), 7481. doi:10.3390/ijerph19127481.

"The Rear Naked Choke - The King of Submissions." n.d. The Jiu Jitsu Brotherhood. Accessed January 31, 2025. https://www.jiujitsubrotherhood.com/blogs/blog/the-rear-naked-choke-the-king-of-submissions.

"Recovering Emotionally from Disaster." 2013. American Psychological Association. Accessed January 31, 2025. https://www.apa.org/topics/disasters-response/recovering.

"Risk of Nuclear Weapons Use Higher Than at Any Time Since Cold War, Disarmament Affairs Chief Warns Security Council." March 31, 2023. United Nations. Accessed January 31, 2025. https://press.un.org/en/2023/sc15250.doc.htm.

Robock, Alan. May/June, 2010. "Nuclear winter." Climate.envsci.rutgers.edu. Accessed January 31, 2025. https://climate.envsci.rutgers.edu/pdf/WiresClimateChangeNW.pdf.

Salter, Charles A. "Psychological Effects of Nuclear and Radiological Warfare." *Military Medicine* 166, no. suppl_2 (December 2001), 17-18. doi:10.1093/milmed/166.suppl_2.17.

Schulze-Makuch, Dirk. November 3, 2022. "Who — or What — Would Survive an All-out Nuclear War?" Big Think. Accessed January 31, 2025. https://bigthink.com/life/who-what-survives-nuclear-war/.

Schwartz, Tony, and Emily Pines. March 23, 2020. "Coping with Fatigue, Fear, and Panic During a Crisis." Harvard Business Review. Accessed January 31, 2025. https://hbr.org/2020/03/coping-with-fatigue-fear-and-panic-during-a-crisis.

"75 Bug Out Bag List Essentials [2024 Update]." Bug Out Bag Academy. Accessed January 31, 2025. https://bugoutbagacademy.com/free-bug-out-bag-list/.

"Shelter-in-Place for Nuclear/Radiological Get In. Stay In. Tune In." November, 2021. US Department of Homeland Security. Accessed January 31, 2025. https://www.fema.gov/sites/default/files/documents/fema_shelter-in-place_guidance-nuclear.pdf.

Siders, Rose. December 28, 2019. "How to Create a Self Care Survival Kit." An Exercise in Frugality. Accessed January 31, 2025. https://anexerciseinfrugality.com/self-care-survival-kit/.

Solis, Karla. February 26, 2017. "12 Survival Games That Teach Your Kids How to Prepare for Emergencies." Survivalcave Inc. Accessed January 31, 2025.

https://www.survivalcavefood.com/blog/teach-kids-survival/?srsltid=AfmBOorlfF8q2Jzgrbu4-2JXx_Qc-GweRbQPJ811qNJoch6b5cNVmaMJ.

Sreenivas, Shishira. March 13, 2024. "How to Handle War Anxiety." WebMD. Accessed January 31, 2025. https://www.webmd.com/mental-health/how-to-handle-war-anxiety.

Stromberg, Joseph. March 13, 2014. "Do You Live Within 50 Miles of a Nuclear Power Plant?" Smithsonian Magazine. Accessed January 31, 2025. https://www.smithsonianmag.com/science-nature/do-you-live-within-50-miles-nuclear-power-plant-180950072/.

Sullivan, Dan F. n.d. "Getting Your Loved Ones to Prepare - Tactics and Tips." The Bug Out Bag Guide. Accessed January 31, 2025. https://www.thebugoutbagguide.com/getting-your-loved-ones-to-prepare/.

"Survival Fitness: Staying Fit and Prepared During an Apocalypse with Limited Food Supply." March 30, 2024. Verdict Restaurant. Accessed January 31, 2025. https://verdictrestaurant.mylocalkfc.com/survival-fitness-staying-fit-and-prepared-during-an-apocalypse-with-limited-food-supply.

"Survival Gardening After Nuclear Fallout." n.d. SurvivalGardenSeeds. Accessed January 31, 2025. https://survivalgardenseeds.com/blogs/survival-garden-training/survival-gardening-after-nuclear-fallout?srsltid=AfmBOorPTjcacR6DmbGRkf6rgi5Z6xXNOlmaBUZX9x7WXZvYxJ-rb9Vs.

"Survival Signals: Off-Grid Communication Strategies You Need." July 17, 2024. Premier Body Armor. Accessed January 31, 2025. https://premierbodyarmor.com/blogs/pba/off-grid-survival-communication-methods?srsltid=AfmBOopLE9QaXoMjnz5Jrpzy_Gyv4pjOUkdfrvWblevPpUcQ8y4ffHCI.

Sutton, Jeremy. December 26, 2024. "How to Be Mentally Strong & Build Mental Toughness." Positive Psychology. Accessed January 31, 2025. https://positivepsychology.com/mentally-strong/.

Swenson, Aaron. July 20, 2022. "5 Best Self-Defense Moves & Techniques for Beginners." FightCamp. Accessed January 31, 2025. https://blog.joinfightcamp.com/training/self-defense-5-effective-moves-for-beginners/.

Swinton, Jonathan. March 20, 2020. "ASK AN EXPERT: Tips for Controlling Fear and Anxiety in a Crisis." Utah State University. Accessed January 31, 2025. https://www.usu.edu/today/story/ask-an-expert-tips-for-controlling-fear-and-anxiety-in-a-crisis.

"Talking to Family About Preparedness: How to Get Your Family to Start Prepping for Disasters." January 13, 2025. Off Grid Survival. Accessed

January 31, 2025. https://offgridsurvival.com/familypreparedness-talkingaboutprepping/.

Taylor, Matthew. November 30, 2021. "Removing Radioactive Contaminants from Water." Save the Water. Accessed January 31, 2025. https://savethewater.org/removing-radioactive-contaminants-from-water/.

"Ten for Survival, Survive Nuclear Attack." 1959. Oak Ridge Associated Universities. Accessed January 31, 2025. https://www.orau.org/health-physics-museum/files/library/civil-defense/ten-for-survival.pdf.

Thomson, Adam, and Paul Ingram. June 19, 2024. "How Would Humans React to Nuclear Catastrophe?" European Leadership Network. Accessed January 31, 2025. https://europeanleadershipnetwork.org/commentary/how-would-humans-react-to-nuclear-catastrophe/.

Thomson, Jess. January 19, 2023. "The Best and Worst Places in a Building If a Nuclear Bomb Goes Off." Newsweek. Accessed January 31, 2025. https://www.newsweek.com/nuclear-bomb-shelter-building-safety-shock-wave-1775021.

Toon, Owen B., Charles G. Bardeen, Alan Robock, Lili Xia, Hans Kristensen, Matthew McKinzie, R. J. Peterson, Cheryl S. Harrison, Nicole S. Lovenduski, and Richard P. Turco. October 2, 2019. "Rapidly expanding nuclear arsenals in Pakistan and India portend regional and global catastrophe." Science Advances. Accessed January 31, 2025. https://www.science.org/doi/10.1126/sciadv.aay5478.

"Top 10 Skills to Help You Survive in a Post-Apocalyptic World." June 11, 2022. Food Bunker. Accessed January 31, 2025. https://foodbunker.co.uk/blogs/prepping/top-10-skills-to-help-you-survive-in-a-post-apocalyptic-world.

"12 Ways to Fortify Your Home Before It's Too Late." May 2, 2021. Tactical.com. Accessed January 31, 2025. https://www.tactical.com/fortify-your-home-shtf/.

"27 Unique DIY Self-Care Kit Ideas for 2023." January 11, 2023. Authentically Del. Accessed January 31, 2025. https://authenticallydel.com/diy-self-care-kit-ideas/.

"US Nuclear Industry." US Energy Information Administration (EIA). Last modified August 24, 2023. https://www.eia.gov/energyexplained/nuclear/us-nuclear-industry.php.

"UK Prepping for Beginners, Step 2: How to Make a Food Stockpile." n.d. Start Prepping UK. Accessed January 31, 2025. https://startprepping.co.uk/uk-prepping-for-beginners-make-a-food-stockpile/.

"The Ultimate Emergency Survival List for Beginner Preppers." July 20, 2021. Project Whim. Accessed January 31, 2025. https://www.projectwhim.com/the-ultimate-emergency-survival-list-for-beginner-preppers/.

"The Ultimate Home Survival Kit (2024 Edition)." October 11, 2024. MIRA Safety. Last modified May 30, 2023. https://www.mirasafety.com/blogs/news/ultimate-home-survival-kit?srsltid=AfmBOooK9mxjvOpTFDuFFH2p6_rm8n-AZRELqLN4mO2FZ8TDLdZz64tK.

"Underground Bunkers, Shelters and Basement Panic Rooms London." n.d. Subterranean Spaces. Accessed January 31, 2025. https://www.subterraneanspaces.co.uk/specialist-basements-bunkers-panic-rooms.

United Nations. n.d. "International Day against Nuclear Tests 29 August." United Nations. Accessed January 31, 2025. https://www.un.org/en/observances/end-nuclear-tests-day/history.

"Use of Potassium Iodine for Thyroid Protection During Nuclear or Radiological Emergencies." July 7, 2023. World Health Organization (WHO). Accessed January 31, 2025. https://www.who.int/news-room/questions-and-answers/item/use-of-potassium-iodine-for-thyroid-protection-during-nuclear-or-radiological-emergencies.

Webber, Philip. n.d. "Nuclear Weapons: a Beginner's Guide to the Threats." Scientists for Global Responsibility. Last modified July 20, 2023. https://www.sgr.org.uk/resources/nuclear-weapons-beginner-s-guide-threats.

Weiner, Liv. December 31, 2018. "Protective Gear During a Nuclear Attack." StemRad. Accessed January 31, 2025. https://stemrad.com/protective-gear/.

"What Do I Do in a Nuclear Emergency?" August 27, 2024. United States Nuclear Regulatory Committee. Accessed January 31, 2025. https://www.nrc.gov/about-nrc/emerg-preparedness/in-radiological-emerg.html.

"What Happens if Nuclear Weapons Are Used?" n.d. ICAN. Accessed January 31, 2025. https://www.icanw.org/catastrophic_harm.

"What to Do and What to Take When Evacuating Your Home." n.d. New Directions. Accessed January 31, 2025. https://www.ndbh.com/Docs/HealthResources/CrisisResources/What_to_do_and_take_when_evacuating_your_home-NDBH.pdf.

"Why Nuclear Energy Is Not Worth the Risk for Australia." January 28, 2025. Climate Council. Accessed January 31, 2025. https://www.climatecouncil.org.au/nuclear-power-stations-are-not-appropriate-for-australia-and-probably-never-will-be/.

Winstead, Daniel J., and Michael G. Jacobson. "Food resilience in a dark catastrophe: A new way of looking at tropical wild edible plants." *Ambio* 51, no. 9 (September 2022), 1949-1962. doi:10.1007/s13280-022-01715-1.

Wolfson, Richard, and Ferenc Dalnoki-Veress. March 2, 2022. "The Devastating Effects of Nuclear Weapons." The MIT Press Reader. Accessed January 31, 2025. https://thereader.mitpress.mit.edu/devastating-effects-of-nuclear-weapons-war/.

Yeung, Jessie, and Emiko Jozuka. August 30, 2022. "Fukushima Town Lifts Evacuation Order 11 Years After Nuclear Disaster." CNN. Last modified August 30, 2022. https://edition.cnn.com/2022/08/30/asia/futaba-fukushima-nuclear-evacuation-order-intl-hnk/index.html.

Young, Taras. March 7, 2019. "The Psychological Impact of Nuclear War." Wellcome Collection. Accessed January 31, 2025. https://wellcomecollection.org/stories/the-psychological-impact-of-nuclear-war.

www.ingramcontent.com/pod-product-compliance
Lightning Source LLC
Chambersburg PA
CBHW022011290426
44109CB00015B/1139